Roger G. Clarke

Options and Futures:
A Tutorial

The Research Foundation of
The Institute of Chartered Financial Analysts

Options and Futures:
A Tutorial

The Research Foundation of AIMR and Blackwell Series in Finance

Roger G. Clarke

Options and Futures:
A Tutorial

The Research Foundation of
The Institute of Chartered Financial Analysts

First published 1992

Reissued in new format by Blackwell Publishers Ltd 2000

2 4 6 8 10 9 7 5 3 1

Blackwell Publishers Inc.
350 Main Street
Malden, Massachusetts 02148
USA

Blackwell Publishers Ltd
108 Cowley Road
Oxford OX4 1JF
UK

Research Foundation of the Association for Investment Management and Research
560 Ray C. Hunt Drive
Charlottesville, Virginia 22903
USA

The Research Foundation of the Association for Investment Management and Research[SM] (AIMR[SM]) does not endorse, promote, review, or warrant the accuracy of the products or services offered by Blackwell Publishers Ltd.

THE RESEARCH FOUNDATION OF THE ASSOCIATION FOR INVESTMENT MANAGEMENT AND RESEARCH™ , THE RESEARCH FOUNDATION OF AIMR™ , and THE RESEARCH FOUNDATION logo are trademarks owned by the Research Foundation of the Association for Investment Management and Research. CFA®, CHARTERED FINANCIAL ANALYST™, AIMR-PPS™, and GIPS™ are just a few of the trademarks owned by the Association for Investment Management and Research. To view a list of the Association for Investment Management and Research's trademarks and a guide for the use of AIMR's marks, please visit the website at www.aimr.org.

This publication is designed to provide accurate and authoritative information in regard to the subject matter covered. It is sold with the understanding that the publisher is not engaged in rendering legal, accounting, or other professional service. If legal advice or other expert assistance is required, the services of a competent professional should be sought.

Library of Congress Cataloging-in-Publication Data is available for this book.

ISBN 0-943205-16-6

British Library Cataloguing in Publication Data
A CIP catalogue record for this book is available from the British Library.

Printed in Great Britain by T.J. International, Padstow, Cornwall

This book is printed on acid-free paper.

Mission

The Research Foundation's mission is to identify, fund, and publish research that is relevant to the AIMR Global Body of Knowledge and useful for AIMR member investment practitioners and investors.

Table of Contents

Acknowledgments

I owe a debt of gratitude to those who have taught me about options and futures over the years. Through the material presented in this volume, I hope to share their efforts with others, although responsibility for any errors herein is solely mine. I also want to acknowledge the funding for this project by the Research Foundation of the Institute of Chartered Financial Analysts. Much of the material presented here has been presented to participants in seminars and conferences sponsored by the Association for Investment Management and Research and has benefitted from their feedback.

A special thanks goes to Barbara Austin, who typed the original manuscript, and to Mindy Cowen, Hadas Perchek, and Lisa Adam, who generated earlier versions of the graphics and illustrations. Finally, an extra special thanks to my family, among others, who waited patiently for me to finally bring this project to a close.

Roger G. Clarke

Foreword

Interest in derivative securities has been growing rapidly since 1973—the year exchange-traded options were introduced in Chicago. The success of the Chicago Board Options Exchange contributed to the proliferation of derivative contracts based on a variety of underlying factors. Options on individual stocks, equity indexes, interest rates, and foreign exchange, for example, are now traded all over the world. Many of the most popular contracts are trading in volumes exceeding those of the underlying elements.

With the growth in derivatives comes a need for all investment practitioners to understand the valuation of these securities and why, how, and when to use them as tools of portfolio management. In response to this need, many books and articles have been published on derivatives and their markets. Some of these publications are textbooks, addressing the fundamentals of the options and futures markets, valuation models, and strategies; others are quite technical, as befits the subject matter.

Clarke adds to this literature a tutorial that provides practical information. It addresses topics that investment practitioners need to know about derivative securities, including what they are, how they trade, how they are priced, and how they are used in portfolio management. The tutorial also discusses the operational advantages and disadvantages of trading in options and futures when compared to trading the underlying securities.

Clearly, one of the biggest contributions of derivative securities is their ability to limit risk (or transfer it to those willing to bear it). Clarke focuses on the risk-control capabilities of options and futures in financial markets, outlining risk-management strategies for each type and explaining the differences among them. He also describes some of the techniques used to monitor option positions and manage exposure in a portfolio. He provides a virtual cookbook on how to fashion such strategies as a covered call, protective put, straddle, and bull call spread.

To give the reader hands-on practice with these techniques, Clarke includes a set of exercises, complete with answers. A glossary provides a handy reference resource for the terms used in this field. Among the appendixes are additional reference materials in the form of a table listing contract specifications for a wide variety of futures contracts, futures options, and index options.

The Research Foundation is proud to publish this, its first, tutorial. We wish to thank Roger Clarke for his important contribution to understanding this complex area of financial analysis and for his assistance in the editorial process. As Clarke notes in his overview of derivative securities and markets, many investors lack the understanding and experience to use futures and options effectively. We hope this tutorial provides an aid in learning to use these securities.

Katrina F. Sherrerd, CFA

1. Overview of Derivative Securities and Markets

The growth in trading of financial options and futures began subsequent to the Chicago Board of Trade's 1973 organization of the Chicago Board Options Exchange (CBOE) to trade standardized option contracts on individual stocks. The success of this market contributed to the growth of other options and futures contracts to the point that many of the most popular contracts are now traded on several different exchanges and in volumes exceeding those of the underlying securities themselves. In addition to options trading on individual stocks, options are also traded in equity indexes, interest rates, and foreign exchange. Table 1.1 shows some of the more popular futures, options, and options on futures contracts. Specifications for selected futures and options contracts are presented in Appendix A.

Options and futures contracts are derivative instruments–derivative because they take their value from their connected underlying security. The relationships between the underlying cash security and its associated options and futures are illustrated in Figure 1.1. In addition, as shown, options may be tied to a future, but all options and futures ultimately derive their value from an underlying cash security.

The links pictured in Figure 1.1 keep the security and its options and futures tightly coupled. The link between the future and the cash security is called *cash-and-carry arbitrage*. The arbitrage linking the options to their underlying security is referred to as *put/call parity*. Both of these arbitrage relationships are discussed in detail in later chapters.

Futures and options share some common characteristics but also have some important differences. The common features of futures and options include (1) standardized contract features, (2) trading on organized exchanges, (3) limited maturity, (4) risk-management capability, and (5) operational efficiencies.

A futures contract is an agreement between a buyer and a seller to trade a security or commodity at a future date. The most popular futures contracts are traded on organized exchanges and have standardized contract specifications relating to how much of the security is to be bought or sold, when the transactions will take place, what features the underlying security must have, and how delivery or transfer of the security is to be handled. To encourage both buyer and seller to follow through with the transaction, a good faith deposit, called *margin*, is usually required from both parties when the contract is initiated.

As the price of the underlying security changes from day to day, the value of the futures contract also changes. The buyer and seller recognize this daily gain or loss by transferring the relative gain to the party reaping the benefit. This practice keeps a large, unrealized loss from accumulating

1

Table 1.1 Selected Derivative Contracts and Exchanges Where Traded

Contract	Futures	Options	Futures Options	Exchange[a]
Indexes				
S&P 500	X	X	X	CME
S&P 100 (OEX)		X		CBOE
Major Market	X	X		CBT, ASE
NYSE Composite	X	X	X	NYFE, NYSE
Value Line	X	X		KC, PH
Institutional		X		ASE
Interest rates				
30-day interest rate	X			CBT
3-month T-bills	X		X	IMM
3-month Eurodollars	X		X	IMM
5-year T-notes	X		X	CBT
10-year T-notes	X		X	CBT
Municipal Bond Index	X		X	CBT
T-bonds	X		X	CBT
Foreign Exchange				
Japanese yen	X	X	X	IMM, PH
Deutsche mark	X	X	X	IMM, PH
Canadian dollar	X	X	X	IMM, PH
British pound	X	X	X	IMM, PH
Swiss franc	X	X	X	IMM, PH
Australian dollar	X	X	X	IMM, PH

[a] CME – Chicago Mercantile Exchange
CBOE – Chicago Board Options Exchange
CBT – Chicago Board of Trade
ASE – American Stock Exchange
IMM – International Monetary Market at the Chicago Mercantile Exchange
KC – Kansas City Board of Trade
PH – Philadelphia Stock Exchange
NYFE – New York Futures Exchange
NYSE – New York Stock Exchange

and reduces the probability of one of the parties defaulting on the obligation.

An option contract possesses many of these same features, but an option differs from a future

Figure 1.1 Arbitrage Links

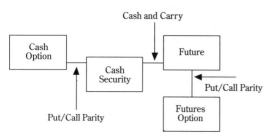

in that the option contract gives the buyer the right, but not the obligation, to purchase or sell a security at a later date at a specified price. The buyer of an option contract has limited liability and can lose, at most, the premium or price paid for the option. The seller of an option has unlimited liability similar to the parties to a futures contract. As a result, the option seller is usually required to post margin, as in a futures contract.

The contracts' standardized features allow futures and options to be traded quickly and efficiently on an organized exchange. The exchange serves as a middleman to facilitate trading, transfer daily gains and losses between parties, and pool resources of exchange members to guarantee financial stability if an investor should default. The exchange's clearinghouse function also allows a buyer or seller to reverse a position before maturity and close out the obligation without having to find the exact party who took the other side of the trade initially. For example, a buyer of a contract merely sells a contract with the same parameters, and the clearinghouse cancels the buyer's original obligation.

Figure 1.2 illustrates the participants in a futures trade. Customers wanting to buy and sell give their orders to a broker or futures commission merchant. These orders are then passed to traders on the exchange floor. Some traders trade for customers' accounts (commission brokers), while others trade for their own accounts (locals). The exchange floor has designated areas, called *pits*, where particular contracts are traded. The trading mechanism is an open-outcry process in which the pit trader offers to buy or sell contracts at an offered price. Other pit traders are free to take the other side of the trade. Once the trade has been agreed upon, the transaction is passed to the exchange clearinghouse, which serves as the bookkeeper to match the trades. The parties to the trade deal with the exchange in settling their gains and losses and handling any physical delivery of the security involved. The two individual parties to the trade need not deal with each other after the exchange has matched the trade of the two parties together. The exchange acts as intermediary and guarantor to handle later settlement duties.

Options trade in a different manner from fu-tures. Instead of an open-outcry system, options trade on the floor of their respective exchanges using a market-maker system. The market maker quotes both a bid and an asked price for the option contract. The floor brokers are free to trade with the market maker or with other floor brokers. The Options Clearing Corporation serves a similar function to the futures exchange clearinghouse in acting as intermediary to match and clear options trades.

The most popular options contracts traded on the exchanges have a specified maturity of from one to nine months. The highest volume of trading, and therefore the most liquidity, usually occurs in the nearest maturity contracts. Settlement between the buyer and seller must take place when or before the contract matures, because the contract has a limited life. After the maturity date, no binding obligation exists to follow through with the transaction.

The use of options and futures gives an investor tremendous flexibility in managing investment risk. Basic investment activity may leave the investor exposed to interest rate, foreign exchange, or equity market risk. The use of options and futures allows an investor to limit or transfer all or some of this risk to others willing to bear it. Although derivative securities can be used in a speculative way, most applications in this tutorial focus on the risk-control capabilities of options and futures with respect to financial assets such as stocks, bonds, and foreign exchange. Active op-

Figure 1.2 Trading Participants

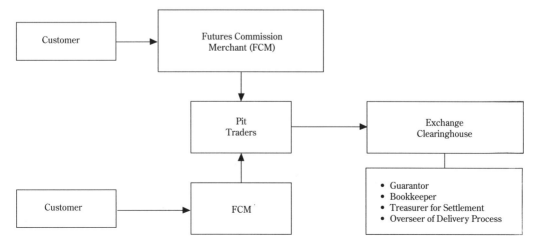

tions and futures contracts do exist, however, for metals and other physical commodities.

Trading in options and futures also has some operational advantages over trading the underlying securities. These include:

- Easy adjustment of market exposure
- Reduction of transaction costs
- Same-day settlement or simultaneous trades
- No disruption of underlying-asset management
- Creation of specialized risk/return patterns

Thus, the use of futures and options allows broad market exposure to be adjusted easily at low transaction costs. In addition, unlike the trade in many underlying cash securities, derivative securities have same-day settlement. Furthermore, derivative securities can be used without the need to buy or sell the underlying securities; therefore, they do not disrupt an existing investment program. Finally, derivative securities can be used to create specialized return patterns.

Using futures and options also has some disadvantages:

- Need to understand complex relationships
- Risk of unfavorable mispricing
- Possibility of tracking error between futures and underlying portfolio
- Liquidity reserve required for margin requirements
- Daily settlement required in marking to market
- Potential short-term tax consequences

Many investors lack the understanding and experience to use futures and options effectively. Futures and options may not track the investor's portfolio exactly or may become slightly mispriced, which causes some tracking error in the investor's strategy. The use of derivative securities does require somewhat more daily attention than do other securities because of the daily mark-to-market and maintenance of cash reserve requirements. Finally, futures and options have a relatively short life, and the closing out of positions may create taxable events more frequently for some investors than they would normally have from a buy-and-hold strategy.

2. Futures Contracts: Pricing Relationships

A futures contract provides an opportunity to contract now for the purchase or sale of an asset or security at a specified price but to delay payment for the transaction until a future settlement date. A futures contract can be either purchased or sold. An investor who purchases a futures contract commits to the purchase of the underlying asset or security at a specified price at a specified date in the future. An investor who sells a futures contract commits to the sale of the underlying asset or security at a specified price at a specified date in the future.

The date for future settlement of the contract is usually referred to as the *settlement* or *expiration date*. The fact that the price is negotiated now but payment is delayed until expiration creates an opportunity cost for the seller in receiving payment. As a result, the negotiated price for future delivery of the asset is usually different from the current cash price in order to reflect the cost of waiting to get paid.

Strictly speaking, such a contract is referred to as a forward contract. A futures contract does contain many of the same elements as a forward contract, but any gains or losses that accrue as the current price of the asset fluctuates relative to the negotiated price in a futures contract are realized on a day-to-day basis. The total gain or loss is generally the same for a futures contract as for a forward contract with the same maturity date,

except that the accumulated gain or loss is realized on a daily basis with the futures contract instead of at the contract's forward settlement date. Futures contracts also usually require the posting of a performance bond with the broker to initiate the trade. The purpose of this bond is to reduce the chance that one of the parties to the trade might build up substantial losses and then default. This performance bond is referred to as *initial margin*. The amount of initial margin varies for different futures contracts, but it usually amounts to between 2 and 10 percent of the contract value. More-volatile contracts usually require higher margins than less-volatile contracts.

Another difference between forward and futures contracts is that futures contracts have standardized provisions specifying maturity date and contract size so they can be traded interchangeably on organized exchanges such as the Chicago Board of Trade or the Chicago Mercantile Exchange. Most contracts that are traded actively are futures contracts, although an active forward market for foreign exchange exists through the banking system. The futures markets are regulated by the Commodity Futures Trading Commission, but active forward markets are not.

Although forward and futures contracts are not the same, this study uses the two terms interchangeably. Research shows that, if interest rates are constant and the term structure is flat, the two will be priced the same (see Cox, Ingersoll, and Ross 1981). These conditions are not met in practice, but the difference in price between a futures and forward contract is usually small (see Cornell and Reinganum 1981, and Park and Chen 1985).

Figure 2.1 diagrams a simple time matrix in reference to futures contracts. At the point labeled "Now," the security and each futures contract have a current price. The current futures price is the price investors agree on for delayed settlement of the purchase or sale of the security at the expiration date. Because futures contracts are usually traded with several different expiration dates, the matrix in Figure 2.1 includes two settlement dates—the "nearby" expiration and the "deferred" expiration dates. When those dates actually arrive, the security itself is likely to have a different price from its present price. A change in the price of the underlying security typically causes the futures price to change also, leaving the futures trader with a gain or a loss. When the nearby expiration date arrives, the nearby contract expires and cannot be traded.

Table 2.1 shows the futures prices quoted for an S&P 500 Index contract with expiration dates staggered over several quarters. The index itself is priced at 394.17, with the more distant expiration dates having increasingly larger settlement prices because the interest opportunity cost is not fully offset by the dividend yield on the stocks in the index. The settlement price for the day reflects the closing trades on the exchange and establishes the price at which the contracts mark to market for margin calculations. The open-interest numbers reflect the number of contracts

Table 2.1 Futures Prices for the S&P 500 Index, August 23, 1991

Expiration Date	Settlement Price	Open Interest	Volume
S&P 500 Index	394.17	—	—
Sep. 1991	394.65	131,640	NA
Dec. 1991	397.40	18,584	NA
Mar. 1992	400.25	1,178	NA
June 1992	404.10	474	NA
		151,876	51,025[a]

Note: NA = Not available by expiration date.
[a]All contract maturities.

of each maturity that have been purchased and are still outstanding (although open interest is typically reported with a one-day lag in newspaper tables). Notice that most of the open interest is found in the nearby contract. The volume of contracts traded during each day is reported in the aggregate and is not usually reported by expiration date. Most of the trading occurs in the first one or two contract maturities, comparable to the pattern in the open-interest figures.

Table 2.2 illustrates the daily marking to market made necessary by daily fluctuations in the futures price. Investors who fail to meet a margin call are subject to having their positions closed out and having their initial margin used to satisfy the daily margin call. In the example using the S&P 500 contract, each point of the index is worth $500. The first day's price move generates a gain of $650 for the buyer of the contract and a $650 loss for the seller. The cumulative gain over the five-day period amounts to $1,075 per contract.

Notice particularly the potential leverage involved in buying or selling a futures contract. The

Figure 2.1 Futures Time Matrix

	Now	Nearby Futures Expiration, t_1	Deferred Futures Expiration, t_2
Security Price =	S	S_{t_1}	S_{t_2}
Nearby Futures Price =	F^1	$F^1_{t_1}$	—
Deferred Futures Price =	F^2	$F^2_{t_1}$	$F^2_{t_2}$

Table 2.2 Daily Variation Margin

Day	S&P 500 Futures Price	Price Change	Gain or Loss	Cumulative Gain or Loss
1	425.05	—	—	—
2	426.35	1.30	$ 650	$ 650
3	424.95	−1.45	−725	−75
4	424.50	−0.40	−200	−275
5	427.20	2.70	1,350	1,075

percentage price change in the futures price itself over the five days is 0.51 percent. If the investor deposits only a $6,000 initial margin with the broker, however, the percentage gain on the initial margin amount is 17.92 percent: A leverage factor of more than 35 to 1 results on the investor's money (17.92/0.51). Depositing a larger amount increases the investor's base and decreases the leverage.

Consequently, futures can be used in a highly leveraged way or in a conservative way, depending on how much the investor commits to the initial margin account. By committing the dollar equivalent of the futures contract initially, the futures contract will generate returns on the investor's funds equivalent to purchasing the underlying security itself. The next section, dealing with the pricing of futures contracts, illustrates why this works.

Pricing a Futures Contract

The price of a futures contract is related to the price of the underlying security or asset, the interest opportunity cost until the date of expiration, and any expected cash distributions by the underlying asset before expiration. The fair pricing of a futures contract is usually derived from the investment position called *cash-and-carry arbitrage*. The arbitrage argument is as follows: Suppose a security with a current price S pays a cash distribution worth C_t at time t and ends with a value of S_t. Table 2.3 shows two different investment strategies that both result in holding the security at time t.

Because both strategies begin with the same dollar investment and result in the investor owning the security at time t, the ending values should also be equal. That is,

$$S_t + C_t = S\left(1 + \frac{rt}{360}\right) + S_t - F.$$

Solving for the futures price gives

$$F = S\left(1 + \frac{rt}{360}\right) - C_t.$$

The price of a futures contract represents the current price of the security adjusted for the opportunity cost of delayed settlement. The seller of the security is compensated for waiting to receive the money by earning interest on the current value of the security. In addition, the futures price is reduced by any cash distributions the seller received before settlement. This adjustment to the security price to arrive at the futures price is sometimes referred to as the *net cost of carry* or *net carry*.

For any given futures price, the investor can infer what interest rate the buyer has to pay to compensate the seller. This rate is usually referred to as the *implied repo rate*. The market tends to price the futures contract such that the implied rate equals a fair-market interest rate. The rate usually varies between the short-term Treasury bill rate and the Eurodollar rate. If the implied

Table 2.3   Cash-and-Carry Arbitrage

Strategy	Value Now	Value at Time t
Strategy I		
Purchase the security	S	$S_t + C_t$
Strategy II		
Invest equivalent $ amount until time t at rate r	S	$S\left(1 + \dfrac{rt}{360}\right)$
Purchase a futures contract on the security for settlement at time t for price F	—	$S_t - F$
Total value for Strategy II	S	$S\left(1 + \dfrac{rt}{360}\right) + S_t - F$

rate is greater than this rate, investors could create a riskless arbitrage to capture the increased return. A rate higher than the market rate could be earned by selling an overvalued futures contract and buying the security. Funds could be borrowed below market rates by buying an undervalued futures contract and selling the security.

To illustrate how the arbitrage works if the implied repo rate is too high, consider the following example:

	Value Now	Value at Time t
Purchase the security	$S = 100$	$S_t + C_t = 96 + 2$
Sell a futures contract	$F = 101$	$F_t = 96$

At expiration ($t = 30$ days), the investor is obligated to sell the security for the futures price F no matter what the final value S_t of the security might be. After taking into account the cash distribution received, the annualized return for t days is

$$r = \left(\frac{F + C_t}{S} - 1\right)\frac{360}{t}$$

$$= \left(\frac{101 + 2}{100} - 1\right)\frac{360}{30}$$

$$= 36 \text{ percent.}$$

At the current futures price, the riskless return created is equal to an annualized rate of 36 percent. Investors would be enticed to sell the futures contract and purchase the security until their relative prices adjusted enough to result in a return more consistent with market interest rates.[1]

Equity Index Futures Pricing. Theoretically, the pricing of an equity index futures con-

tract is established according to the following formula:

$$F = \text{Index} + \text{Interest} - \text{Dividend income}$$

$$= S\left(1 + \frac{rt}{360}\right) - D,$$

where

- F = fair value futures price,
- S = equity index,
- r = annualized financing rate (money-market yield),
- D = value of dividends paid before expiration, and
- t = days to expiration.

Because dividend yields are often less than short-term interest rates, the futures price is often greater than the index price.

Consider, as an example, a contract on the S&P 500 Index that is traded on the Chicago Mercantile Exchange with quarterly expiration dates ending in March, June, September, and December. The size of the contract is equal to $500 times the value of the S&P 500 Index. The contract does not require the purchase or sale of actual shares of stock but is settled in cash equivalent to the value of the shares. Assume the index is at 420, and the expiration time for the contract is 84 days. The financing rate is 6.6 percent a year, and expected dividends through expiration in index points are 2.24. Thus, according to the general form for the price of an equity futures contract,

$$F = 420\left[1 + \frac{(0.066 \times 84)}{360}\right] - 2.24 = 424.23.$$

If the actual futures price is quoted at 423.95, the future appears to be underpriced by 0.28 index points relative to fair value.

The repo rate implied by the actual price is given by

$$r = \left[\frac{F + D}{S} - 1\right]\frac{360}{t}$$

$$= \left[\frac{423.95 + 2.24}{420} - 1\right]\frac{360}{84}$$

$$= 6.3 \text{ percent.}$$

---

[1] For some securities or commodities, selling the futures contract is easier than shorting the underlying security. This can create an asymmetry in the arbitrage conditions. The futures price rarely goes to excess on the upside, but it sometimes goes to excess on the downside because creating the downside arbitrage by buying the futures contract and selling the security is more difficult. Thus, futures prices are more easily underpriced relative to their fair value, as indicated by implied repo rates that are less than market riskless rates.

Whether this mispricing is large enough to take advantage of depends on how expensive it would be actually to create the arbitrage position after transaction costs are taken into account.

Bond Futures Pricing. The pricing of a bond futures contract is somewhat more complicated than for an equity index contract:

$$F = \text{(Price + Interest cost}$$

$$- \text{Coupon income)/Delivery factor}$$

$$= \frac{P\left(1 + \dfrac{rt}{360}\right) - Bc\dfrac{(t+a)}{365}}{f},$$

where

B = par value of the cheapest-to-deliver bond,
P = market price of bond B + accrued interest,
r = annualized financing rate (money-market yield),
c = annualized coupon rate,
t = days to expiration,
a = days of accrued interest, and
f = delivery factor of bond B.

For example, consider a Treasury bond futures contract with 98 days to expiration that is traded on the Chicago Board of Trade with quarterly expiration dates ending in March, June, September, and December. The size of the contract is equal to $100,000 face value of eligible Treasury bonds having at least 15 years to maturity and not callable for at least 15 years. The contract requires the purchase or sale of actual Treasury bonds if it is held to expiration.

Because different bonds have different coupon payments and different maturities, the actual Treasury bond selected for delivery by the short seller is adjusted in price by a delivery factor to reflect a standardized 8 percent coupon rate. This adjustment normalizes the Treasury bonds eligible for delivery so that the short seller has some flexibility in choosing which bond might actually be delivered to make good on the contract. The factor associated with any bond is calculated by dividing by 100 the dollar price that the bond would command if it were priced to yield 8 percent to maturity (or to first call date). The pricing of the futures contract generally follows the price of the

bond cheapest to deliver at the time. The futures price itself is quoted in 32nds, with 100 being the price of an 8 percent coupon bond when its yield to maturity is also equal to 8 percent.

The fair price of the Treasury bond futures contract is also adjusted by the interest opportunity cost ($Prt/360 = 1 13/32$) and the size of the coupon payments up to the expiration date of the futures contract $[Bc(t+a)/365] = 2 5/32$.[2] Thus, the theoretical price of the bond future is:

Market price (7.25% of 2016)	78⁵⁄₃₂
+ Interest cost	1¹³⁄₃₂
− Coupon income	−2⁵⁄₃₂
	77¹³⁄₃₂
÷ Delivery factor	0.9167
= Theoretical futures price	84¹⁴⁄₃₂

The actual price of this contract is 84¹²⁄₃₂, a mispricing that is equal to −²⁄₃₂.

If the short-term interest rate is less than the coupon rate on the cheapest-to-deliver (CTD) bond, the futures price will be less than the bond's price. If the short-term interest rate is greater than the coupon rate on the bond, the futures price will be greater than the bond's price. Because short-term rates are generally lower than long-term rates, the futures price is often less than the bond's price.

Eurodollar Futures Pricing. Eurodollar futures are another popular futures contract. They are traded on several exchanges, but most of the trading volume occurs at the International Monetary Market at the Chicago Mercantile Exchange. Eurodollar futures have the same monthly expiration dates (March, June, September, and December) as do futures on Treasury notes and bonds. These contracts are settled in cash, and each contract corresponds to a $1 million deposit with a three-month maturity. Eurodollar futures are quoted as an index formed by subtracting from 100 the percentage forward rate for the three-month London Interbank Offered Rate (LIBOR) at the date of expiration of the contract.

---

[2] Treasury note futures contracts are priced in the same way as Treasury bond contracts except the eligible notes for delivery must have at least 6½ years to maturity at the time of delivery.

The pricing formula for a Eurodollar futures contract is

$$F = 100(1 - f_t),$$

where f_t is the annualized three-month LIBOR forward rate beginning at time t. For example, if $f_t = 7.31$ percent and $t = 35$ days, the futures price would be quoted as 92.69.

This type of price quotation does not appear to have the same arbitrage conditions as the other contracts. The arbitrage process, however, is working to keep these forward interest rates consistent with the implied forward rates in the market term structure of interest rates. A short review of interest rate relationships and forward rates is given in Appendix B.

Treasury Bill Futures Pricing. Futures on three-month Treasury bills are also traded at the International Monetary Market. The futures contracts have the same maturity months as the Treasury notes and bonds and the Eurodollar contracts, and have a face value of $1 million. Settlement at expiration involves delivery of the current three-month Treasury bill. The Treasury bill future is quoted the same way as the Eurodollar future. The forward interest rate used to calculate the index, however, is the three-month forward discount rate on Treasury bills at the expiration date of the futures contract.

The price for such contracts is calculated as follows:

$$F = 100(1 - d_t),$$

where d_t is the annualized three-month forward discount rate on a Treasury bill beginning at time t. For example, if $d_t = 8.32$ percent and $t = 45$ days, the futures price would be quoted as 91.68.

The volume of Treasury bill futures traded has been declining in recent years, and the volume of Eurodollar futures has been increasing. The Eurodollar future is now the more liquid contract.

Foreign Currency Futures Pricing. Futures contracts in foreign currencies are traded at the International Monetary Market with the same expiration cycle of March, June, September, and December. Each contract has an associated size relative to the foreign currency; for example,

Currency	Contract Size
British pound	62,500
Canadian dollar	100,000
French franc	250,000
Japanese yen	12,500,000
Deutsche mark	125,000
Swiss franc	125,000
Australian dollar	100,000

Settlement at expiration involves a wire transfer of the appropriate currency two days after the last trading day.

The fair pricing of a foreign exchange futures contract follows the same arbitrage process as that of the other futures contracts resulting in the relationship:

$$F = \frac{S\left(1 + \dfrac{r_d t}{360}\right)}{\left(1 + \dfrac{r_f t}{360}\right)},$$

where r_f is the foreign interest rate, r_d is the domestic interest rate, and S is the spot exchange rate. An opportunity cost exists at the domestic interest rate, while the foreign currency has an opportunity cost at the foreign interest rate. This arbitrage relationship is often called *covered interest arbitrage.*

To understand this relationship, consider the following investments. In the first case, the investor invests one unit of the domestic currency for t days at an annual rate of r_d. As an alternative, the investor could convert the domestic currency to the foreign currency at a spot exchange rate of S ($/foreign currency), receive interest at the foreign interest rate, and then contract to convert back to the domestic currency at the forward foreign exchange rate F. Each investment is essentially riskless, so both strategies should result in the same value at time t. Equating the two values gives

$$\left(1 + \frac{r_d t}{360}\right) = \frac{F\left(1 + \dfrac{r_f t}{360}\right)}{S}.$$

The forward foreign exchange rate would have to be set at its fair value in order for both strategies to give the same rate of return. If the forward exchange rate deviated from this fair value, the difference could be arbitraged to give profits with no risk. Solving for the appropriate forward exchange rate from the equation above gives

$$F = \frac{S\left(1 + \frac{r_d t}{360}\right)}{\left(1 + \frac{r_f t}{360}\right)}.$$

The calculation of a fair forward exchange rate, given interest rates in Japan and the United States and using the covered interest rate arbitrage relationship is shown below. Assume the Japanese interest rate is 3.5 percent, the U.S. interest rate is 4.2 percent, and the time to expiration is 35 days. The exchange rate is .00799 dollars per yen or 125.16 yen per dollar. That is,

$$F = \frac{0.00799\left(1 + \frac{1.47}{360}\right)}{\left(1 + \frac{1.22}{360}\right)} = 0.00800\$/yen, \text{ or}$$

$$F = \frac{1}{0.00800} = 125.07 yen/\$.$$

The futures price reflects the relative difference in interest rates between countries over the time period. The lower foreign interest rate results in a higher forward exchange rate for future delivery.

Basis and Calendar Spread Relationships

The fair price of a futures contract based on the elimination of arbitrage opportunities results in the futures price being a function of the current spot price and the interest opportunity cost until expiration, less any expected cash distribution received from the security through the expiration date. The futures price is not necessarily a good predictor of what spot prices will be at the expiration date. The futures price is related to the expected future spot price through its dependence on the current spot price plus the net carrying cost. For some securities, the futures price is lower than the current spot price of the security, and for others it is higher than the current spot

Figure 2.2   Value as a Function of Security Price

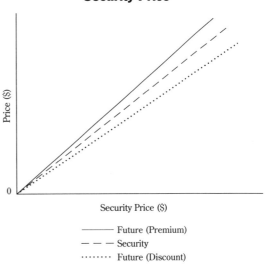

price. Figure 2.2 illustrates these two relationships. Notice particularly that the relationship between the futures price and the security price is a linear one across the full range of the underlying security price. This linear relationship is one of the things that distinguishes the futures contract from an option. The option value has a nonlinear relationship with the security price, which gives it quite different characteristics from the futures contract.

Figure 2.3 illustrates the relationships between the spot and the futures prices and between two futures prices with different expiration dates. This

Figure 2.3   Spot and Futures Prices

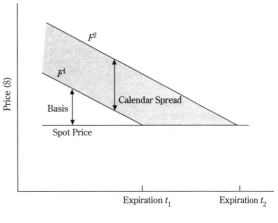

11

difference between the spot and futures prices is usually referred to as the *basis*. The theoretical basis is a function of the difference between any anticipated cash distributions from the underlying security and the interest opportunity cost.[3] That is,

$$\text{Basis} = S - F$$

$$= C_t - \frac{Srt}{360}.$$

As the future draws closer and closer to expiration, the sizes of both the potential cash distributions and the interest opportunity cost decline. This decline forces the basis toward zero at expiration. Such narrowing of the basis is called *convergence*. The futures and spot prices gradually converge as the expiration date approaches in such a way that, at expiration, the two prices are the same. The futures price for same-day delivery is the spot price.

A *calendar spread* is the difference in price between two futures contracts with different expiration dates. The theoretical calendar spread is a function of the difference in anticipated cash distributions and the difference in interest opportunity costs between the two expiration dates using current interest rates with the appropriate maturities $(t_2 > t_1)$.[4] That is,

$$\text{Calendar spread} = F^1 - F^2$$

$$= (C_2 - C_1) - \frac{S(r_2 t_2 - r_1 t_1)}{360}.$$

Not surprisingly, the theoretical calendar spread between two contracts is related to the forward interest rate between the two contract expiration dates $({}_1 f_2)$. The forward interest rate relationship between two dates is given by:

$$\left(1 + \frac{r_2 t_2}{360}\right) = \left(1 + \frac{r_1 t_1}{360}\right)\left[1 + \frac{{}_1 f_2(t_2 - t_1)}{360}\right],$$

---

[3] For some contracts—those that are usually priced at a premium relative to the security price (such as the S&P Index contract)—the basis is sometimes quoted as $F - S$. This approach allows the basis to be positive, which is sometimes easier for investors to work with than a negative number.

[4] Similar to the basis calculation, contracts typically priced at a premium relative to the spot price often calculate the calendar spread by calculating $F^2 - F^1$, which generally keeps the spreads positive.

where r_1 is the current interest rate of maturity t_1, and r_2 is the current interest rate of maturity t_2. Substituting this relationship into the equation for the calendar spread gives

$$F^1 - F^2 = (C_2 - C_1)$$

$$- \frac{S\left(1 + \frac{r_1 t_1}{360}\right) {}_1 f_2(t_2 - t_1)}{360}.$$

Figure 2.3 illustrates the basis and calendar-spread relationships graphically. As the expiration date of each contract approaches, the basis gradually converges to zero, while the calendar spread maintains a more or less constant gap. Any change in the spread relationship is sensitive to a change in the forward interest rate between t_1 and t_2.

To understand these relationships, consider the following example of S&P 500 futures contracts with the Index at 425.05. Assume that the nearby contract expires in 78 days and the deferred contract expires in 168 days. Also assume that the respective interest rates with those maturities are 6.9 percent and 7.1 percent. Dividends on the S&P 500 Index are expected to total 2.11 in index points before the nearby expiration and 4.55 before the deferred contract expiration.

The fair futures price for each contract is

$$F^1 = S\left(1 + \frac{r_1 t_1}{360}\right) - C_1$$

$$= 425.05\left[1 + 0.069\left(\frac{78}{360}\right)\right] - 2.11$$

$$= 429.29, \text{ and}$$

$$F^2 = S\left(1 + \frac{r_2 t_2}{360}\right) - C_2$$

$$= 425.05\left[1 + 0.071\left(\frac{168}{360}\right)\right] - 4.55$$

$$= 434.58.$$

The fair basis for each contract is

$F^1 - S = 429.29 - 425.05 = 4.24$, and

$F^2 - S = 434.58 - 425.05 = 9.53$.

The fair calendar spread is

$F^2 - F^1 = 434.58 - 429.29 = 5.29$.

The forward rate implied by the fair calendar spread is

$$_1f_2 = \frac{(F^2 - F^1) + (C_2 - C_1)}{S\left(1 + \dfrac{r_1 t_1}{360}\right)\left(\dfrac{t_2 - t_1}{360}\right)}$$

$$= \frac{5.29 + (4.55 - 2.11)}{425.05\left[1 + 0.069\left(\dfrac{78}{360}\right)\right]\left[\dfrac{(168 - 78)}{360}\right]}$$

$= 7.2$ percent.

3. Risk Management Using Futures Contracts: Hedging

Depending on the investment base, futures can be used in a very leveraged way, or they can be used in a more moderate way. This chapter focuses on the use of futures in a moderate way to control the risk of an investment position. The chapter begins with a section describing a simple framework to hedge an investment position that illustrates the general characteristics of hedging. A subsequent section discusses specific hedging applications in a general framework.

Net Price Created by a Hedge

Suppose an investor currently holds an asset valued at S and sells a futures contract to hedge its price movement. At time t, the security is worth S_t, and the current price of the futures contract F has a price F_t at time t:

	Security	Future	Basis
Now	S	F	$S - F$
Time t	S_t	F_t	$S_t - F_t$

What is the value of the hedged position at time t? Because the hedged position is formed by holding the underlying security and selling the futures contract, the value of the hedged position (V_t) at time t is equal to the price of the underlying security at time t plus the gain or loss on the futures contract; that is,

$$V_t = S_t + (F - F_t)$$
$$= \text{Ending security price} + \text{Futures gain}.$$

A rearrangement of these terms gives the value of the hedged position at time t in two other equivalent forms:

$$V_t = F + (S_t - F_t)$$
$$= \text{Initial futures price} + \text{Ending basis}$$

$$= S + [(S_t - F_t) - (S - F)]$$
$$= \text{Initial security price} + \text{Change in basis}.$$

The second of these three forms suggests another way to think about the value of the position created by hedging is that it is equal to the initial futures price plus the basis at time t. The third form suggests the value of the hedged position can be thought of as the initial price of the security plus the change in the basis between now and time t. These equations are equivalent ways of expressing the value an investor creates by hedging an underlying security using a futures contract.

One of the most intuitive interpretations of the three expressions relative to the notion of hedging is the second, in which the value of the hedged position is equal to the current price of the futures contract plus the basis at time t. An investor who sells a futures contract agrees to sell the underlying asset at the then-current futures price. If the time horizon for the hedge is equal to the expiration date of the future, the basis is generally zero,

15

so the value of the hedged position is equal to the current futures price no matter what happens to the price of the underlying security in the meantime. The investor has created a riskless position by holding the underlying security and selling a futures contract. If the hedge horizon is less than the time to expiration of the futures contract, the net carrying cost for the actual holding period is different from that implied in the current futures price. Consequently, in the calculation of the value of the hedged position, the value differs from the price of the current futures contract by the remaining portion of the net carrying cost reflected in the basis at time t. A hedged position thus reduces the fundamental price risk in the underlying security to just the price risk in the basis. As a result, hedging is sometimes referred to as *speculation in the basis*.

Alternatively, the investor can think of the value of the hedged position as equal to the current price of the security being hedged plus the change in the basis between now and time t. The convergence of the futures contract toward the security price makes the value differ from the current cash price of the security by the convergence in the basis.

When an investor already holds the underlying security and sells a futures contract to hedge the price risk, this type of hedge is often referred to as an *inventory hedge*. An alternative formulation of a simple hedging framework, which yields exactly the same interpretation, is referred to as an *anticipatory hedge*. In an anticipatory hedge, an investor purchases a futures contract now instead of purchasing the underlying cash security. At time t, the investor then purchases the security and sells the futures contract (to close out the position). The net price (P_t) the investor will have paid for the ending security position at time t will be equal to the security price at time t less the gain or loss on the futures position. This expression is the same as the value of the hedged position for an inventory hedge developed previously, in which the net price equals the ending security price minus the futures gain; that is,

$$P_t = S_t - (F_t - F).$$

Rewriting the net price in two additional ways shows that the investor can think of the net price paid for the security as being equal to the current futures price plus the ending basis:

$$P_t = F + (S_t - F_t),$$

or equivalently, as equal to the current security price plus the change in basis:

$$P_t = S + [(S_t - F_t) - (S - F)].$$

An investor who takes a position in the futures market now in anticipation of converting that position into the underlying security at time t essentially creates the same price as one who buys the security now and hedges the price risk. The two strategies are mirror images because both make a commitment now to buy or sell the underlying security at time t. The price the market is offering the investor for delayed settlement of the transaction is the same for both strategies and is given by the current futures price.

To illustrate a simple hedging situation, consider this example: Suppose an investor expects to have cash to purchase 90-day Eurodollars in two months but wants to enter into the transaction now. Fearing that interest rates may fall between now and then, the investor decides to hedge by purchasing Eurodollars futures now. What is the net price the investor pays? The market offers a futures price of 93.20, or 6.80 percent. Current Eurodollar rates implied by the spot price of 92.80 are 7.2 percent. In two months, rates have fallen to 5.3 percent and the futures price has risen by 1.60, so the investor closes out the futures position for a gain. This gain serves to increase the net rate the investor will receive on the Eurodollar investment from the then-current rate of 5.3 percent to 6.9 percent. Using the equations for net price,

	Cash	Future	Basis
Now	92.80	93.20	−0.40
Two months later	94.70	94.80	−0.10
Net change	1.90	1.60	0.30

P_t = Ending cash price − Futures gain
  = 94.70 − 1.60
  = Beginning futures price + Ending basis
  = 93.20 − 0.10
  = Beginning cash price + Change in basis
  = 92.80 + 0.30
  = 93.10, or 6.90 percent.

In summary, the price the hedger receives when constructing an inventory hedge for an existing security position or when constructing an anticipatory hedge for an anticipated position is equal to the current futures price plus whatever the basis is at the termination of the hedge. When dealing with interest rate hedging, the hedger can lock in the interest rate implied by the futures contract (the forward rate) but cannot lock in the current interest rate (unless the forward rate happens to equal the current rate). The hedger cannot guarantee receipt of the current spot price (or interest rate) unless settlement takes place now. Any promise of delayed settlement is done at a price offered by the market for delayed settlement (the futures price), which is not usually equal to the current spot price unless the net cost of carry is zero.

Synthetic Securities

Another way to think about the use of futures contracts is to realize that the cash-and-carry arbitrage process ensures that the futures contract plus a cash reserve behaves like the underlying security; that is,

$$\text{Future} + \text{Cash} \leftrightarrow \text{Security.}$$

At times, an investor may wish to create the same risk/return profile as a security but use a futures contract. As noted earlier, making the transaction in the futures market can often be done more quickly and at less cost than buying or selling the underlying security.

Table 3.1 illustrates the parallel performance of the underlying security and the synthetic security created by using the futures market and a cash reserve. In this case, the equity index, which was 321.63, has fallen to 310.60, or −3.4 percent, during the course of a month. If the investor had put the same dollar amount in a cash reserve paying 6 percent and purchased a futures contract,

Table 3.1   Synthetic Equity: Futures Example

Item	Price Now	Price 1 Month Later	Percentage Change
Cash reserve	321.63	323.24[a]	0.5
Equity future	323.05	311.05	−3.7
Value of cash + Futures position	321.63	311.24[b]	−3.2

[a]321.63 (1 + 0.06/12) = 323.24.
[b]323.24 − (323.05 − 311.05) = 311.24

the synthetic security would have resulted in a return of −3.2 percent. The −3.2 percent return is composed of a 0.5 percent return on the cash reserve for one month and a −3.7 percent price change on the equity futures contract. The arbitrage between the futures contract and the underlying index keeps the futures price in a relationship such that the total returns will be similar. Small differences can sometimes occur, as in this case, because of tracking error between the index and the futures contract.

In addition to the creation of a synthetic security, rewriting the basic arbitrage relationship to create synthetic cash is sometimes useful. Creating a synthetic cash position is nothing more than creating a hedged position:

$$\text{Security} - \text{Future} \leftrightarrow \text{Cash.}$$

The cash-and-carry arbitrage relationship keeps the future priced so that an offsetting position in the futures contract relative to the underlying security results in a return consistent with a riskless rate.

In essence, creating a hedged position is an attempt to eliminate the primary risk in the underlying security and shift it to others in the futures market willing to bear the risk. The risk can always be shifted by eliminating the underlying security position, but this may interfere with the nature of the investor's business or disrupt a continuing investment program. The futures market often provides an alternate way to control or eliminate much of the risk in the underlying security position.

Table 3.2 shows the effect of hedging the risk in an underlying equity portfolio that tracks the S&P 500 Index. Suppose that over the course of a month, the S&P 500 Index falls by 3.4 percent, and the future falls by 3.7 percent as a result, in part, of the one-month convergence of the futures price. If the entire portfolio were hedged, the net portfolio return would be 0.3 percent for the month, excluding any dividend yield. If half the portfolio were hedged, the net portfolio return would be −1.5 percent, compared with a price change of −3.4 percent for the S&P 500. Using the futures market allows an investor to eliminate some or all of the price risk in the equity portfolio, the equivalent of altering the beta of the portfolio. A partial hedge would reduce the beta below 1,

Table 3.2 Hedging Equity Risk: Futures Example

Item	Price Now	Price 1 Month Later	Percentage Change
Equity future	323.05	311.05	−3.7
Equity index	321.63	310.60	−3.4
Basis	1.42	0.45	

Proportion of Portfolio Hedged	Net Portfolio Return (%)	Relative Portfolio Risk (beta)
0.0	−3.4	1.0
0.25	−2.5	0.75
0.50	−1.5	0.50
0.75	−0.6	0.25
1.00	0.3	0.0

and a complete hedge would reduce the beta to zero.

A different way of looking at the creation of synthetic cash is to calculate the implied repo rate in the pricing of the futures contract itself. As an example, consider a situation in which

S&P 500 Index (S) = 321.63,

S&P future (F) = 323.05,

Days to expiration (t) = 37, and

Dividends (D) = 0.93.

$$r = \left(\frac{F + D}{S} - 1\right)\frac{360}{t}$$

$$= (0.0073)(9.73)$$

$$= 7.1 \text{ percent.}$$

Thus, the implied repo rate in the futures contract is 7.1 percent. If the current Treasury bill rate with a maturity of 37 days is 6.6 percent, the futures contract would be slightly overpriced. In theory, an investor can capture the higher rate of return over the 37-day period by selling the overpriced futures contract and purchasing the stocks in the index. In practice, the differential needs to be large enough to more than cover the transaction costs of buying and selling.

The impact of hedging can also be seen by examining the effect of hedging on a portfolio's return profile and probability distribution. Figure 3.1 illustrates the return on the hedged portfolio

Figure 3.1 Return Profiles for Hedged Portfolios

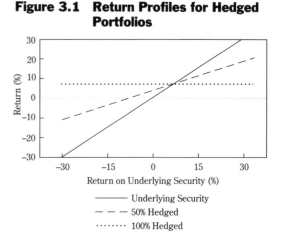

relative to the return on the underlying security. A partial hedge position reduces the slope of the return line, so the hedged portfolio does not perform as well as the underlying security when returns are high, but it also does not perform as poorly when returns are low. The slope of the line is comparable to the beta of an equity portfolio. The greater the portion of the portfolio hedged, the less slope the line will have. A full hedge produces a flat line, indicating that the hedged portfolio will generate a fixed return no matter what the underlying asset does. This fixed return should be equal to the riskless rate if the future is fairly priced.

Figure 3.2 shows how the futures hedge changes the probability distribution of returns. If the return distribution for the underlying security is symmetrical with a wide dispersion, hedging the

Figure 3.2 Return Distributions for Hedged Portfolios

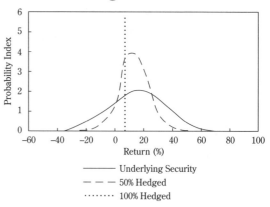

portfolio with futures gradually draws both tails of the distribution in toward the middle, and the mean return shrinks back somewhat toward the riskless rate. A full hedge draws both tails into one place and puts all of the probability mass at the riskless rate.

Hedging with futures generally affects both tails equally. One of the main differences between options and futures is that options can affect one tail more dramatically than the other, so the distribution becomes quite skewed. Figure 3.3 illustrates the difference in the return distributions caused by a partial futures hedge versus a partial hedge created by using a put option.

Figure 3.3   Return Distributions for Hedged Portfolios

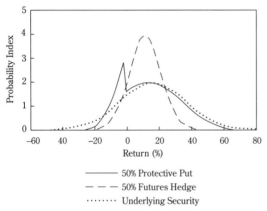

――――― 50% Protective Put
― ― ― 50% Futures Hedge
········· Underlying Security

The Choice of Contract Maturity

An additional issue a hedger must consider is what maturity of futures contract to use in constructing the hedge position. If the hedging horizon T extends beyond the expiration of the nearby futures contract at time t_1, the hedger must use the longer maturity futures contract at some point in order to maintain the hedge. Thus, the investor has a choice of initiating the hedge by using the nearby contract and rolling forward into a deferred one (a *strip*) or using only a deferred contract (a *stack*) from the beginning.

Rolling the contract forward requires that an investor sell one maturity contract and buy the other at time $t \leq t_1$. Figure 3.4 illustrates the time frame for the construction of the hedge. If the hedge horizon is longer than the expiration of the nearby futures contract, an investor who initiates

Figure 3.4   Hedging Time Frame

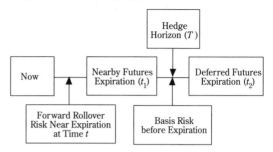

a hedge with the nearby contract is exposed to the price risk of rolling the nearby contract over into the deferred contract before the expiration date t_1. An investor who uses only the deferred contract is not exposed to forward rollover risk.

Figure 3.5 illustrates the difference between the contract positions needed for the stack and for the strip. A hedge created using the deferred contract initially stacks all the contract positions into the deferred maturity. These positions can be

Figure 3.5   Stack vs. Strip: Contract Positions

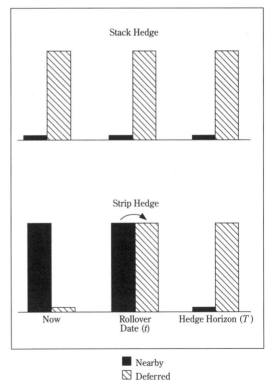

■ Nearby
▨ Deferred

maintained throughout the course of the hedge, and no further changes need be made in the positions. A hedge created using the nearby contract first places all the contracts in the nearby contract and then rolls them forward into the deferred contract before the nearby contract expires at time t_1. What the calendar spread will be at the point of the forward roll is uncertain, and therefore, the price that the hedger creates with a strip will have some uncertainty in addition to the uncertainty of the basis at the time the hedge is terminated.

Consider the net price received if a stack is chosen. Using only the deferred contract, the resulting net price for the hedger is a function of the gain on the deferred contract or, equivalently, is equal to the current futures price on the deferred contract plus the ending basis. The only uncertainty is caused by the uncertainty of the basis at the termination of the hedge:

$$P_T \text{ (stack)} = S_T - (F_T^2 - F^2)$$

$$= F^2 + (S_T - F_T^2).$$

If the nearby contract is used first to create a strip hedge and then rolled into the deferred contract at time $t \leq t_1$, the net price will be a function of the gain or loss on both contracts. An equivalent way of thinking about the net price of the strip is that it is equal to the current futures price on the nearby contract less the calendar spread at the point of the roll plus the ending basis. There are two sources of uncertainty—the risk of the calendar roll, and the basis at termination:

$$P_T \text{ (strip)} = S_T - (F_t^1 - F^1) - (F_T^2 - F_t^2)$$

$$= F^1 - (F_t^1 - F_t^2) + (S_T - F_T^2).$$

The difference between the net price of the stack versus the strip depends on the calendar spread between the two contracts at the point of the forward roll at time t relative to the spread now:

$$P_T \text{ (stack)} - P_T \text{ (strip)} = (F_t^1 - F_t^2) - (F^1 - F^2).$$

The strip results in a lower net price to the hedger if the calendar spread at the point of the roll is smaller than at the initiation of the hedge. The strip gives the hedger the chance to roll into the longer maturity contract at a smaller spread, but it also entails the risk that the spread may be larger.

Because the calendar spread is a function of the forward interest rates, using the strip exposes the hedge to interest rate risk at time t.

As an illustration of this type of risk, consider the following prices for two S&P 500 futures contracts at the forward roll date (t) and the hedge termination date (T):

	Now	t	T
S&P 500 (S)	360.25	375.20	370.15
Near contract (F^1)	363.05	375.45	—
Next contract (F^2)	365.95	378.20	371.05

The net price using a stacked hedge is

$$P_T \text{ (stack)} = S_T - (F_T^2 - F^2) = 365.05.$$

The net price using the stripped hedge is

$$P_T \text{ (strip)} = S_T - (F_t^1 - F^1) - (F_T^2 - F_t^2)$$

$$= 364.90.$$

The difference between the two prices is caused by the change in the calendar spread between the initiation of the hedge and the forward roll at time t:

$$(F_t^1 - F_t^2) - (F^1 - F^2) = -2.75 + 2.90 = 0.15.$$

The stripped hedge is slightly cheaper after the fact because the calendar spread at the point of the forward roll was cheaper by 0.15 index points than it was at the initiation of the hedge.

A Generalized Hedging Framework

The previous section presented a simple hedging framework to illustrate the basics of using a generic futures contract to hedge a position in an underlying security. The simple framework assumed that one contract was the appropriate position to take in hedging the underlying security position. Equal dollar exposure in the futures contract may not, however, create the optimal hedge. This section discusses hedging in a general framework that can accommodate complex situations and explores the details of different contracts on specific underlying securities.

To set up the generalized framework, suppose an investor wants to hedge the value of a security over the short term with a futures position. The hedge position would be formed by holding the underlying security plus h futures contracts:

$$V = S + hF,$$

where S represents the security price, F is the futures price, and h is the hedge ratio.

The change in the value of the hedged position as the security price changes is

$$\Delta V = \Delta S + h\Delta F.$$

Solving for the hedge ratio gives

$$h = \frac{\Delta V - \Delta S}{\Delta F}.$$

For a complete, or delta-neutral hedge ($\Delta V = 0$),[5] the hedge ratio would be

$$h = \frac{-\Delta S}{\Delta F}.$$

A simple hedge is given in the following example, in which S is a diversified equity portfolio, F is an S&P 500 future, and $\Delta S/\Delta F$ is assumed to equal 0.91, indicating that the equity portfolio is somewhat less risky than the S&P 500. For a complete hedge, the hedge ratio is

$$h = \frac{-\Delta S}{\Delta F} = -0.91.$$

An investor would sell futures contracts worth 91 percent of the value of the equity portfolio. If the investor wanted only a partial hedge ($\Delta V = 0.6\Delta S$), the hedge ratio is

$$h = \frac{\Delta V - \Delta S}{\Delta F} = -0.36.$$

---

[5] Strictly speaking, this application of a delta-neutral hedge incorporates only a change in price over the very short term and does not adjust for any convergence in the futures price resulting from the passage of time. Allowing for the passage of time in the delta-neutral hedge would suggest that $\Delta V = Sr\Delta t/360$ instead of zero.

The investor would sell futures contracts worth only 36 percent of the value of the equity portfolio.

Because the equity portfolio does not move one for one with the S&P 500 futures contract, the investor does not want to use a hedge ratio of -1 to hedge the equity risk in the underlying securities. A delta-neutral hedge requires fewer futures contracts to be used, because the underlying equity portfolio has only 91 percent of the movement of the futures contract. In this case, the hedge ratio of -0.91 indicates that the investor sells futures contracts worth 91 percent of the value of the equity portfolio. This process is sometimes called a *cross hedge*, because the futures contract does not perfectly replicate the price movement of the underlying securities. A hedge can still be created, but the link between price movements in the futures contract and the underlying security position may not be tight, which leaves some chance for residual noise in the relationship.

The example given above also shows what the hedge ratio must be if only a partial hedge is created to protect against the price movement in the underlying securities. If the combined hedged position is targeted to have 60 percent of the movement of the underlying securities, a hedge ratio of -0.36 is needed. The investor would sell futures contracts worth only 36 percent of the value of the equity portfolio to create the partial hedge.

Table 3.3 lists the alternatives usually discussed in formulating complete hedge ratios. The equal-dollar-matched hedge ratio is a simple and quick alternative, but it is only a special case of the more general framework, which tries to minimize the tracking error in the hedge. This hedge ratio, which minimizes the variance of the hedged value, is referred to as the minimum-variance hedge ratio. The regression technique is sometimes used to estimate the minimum-variance hedge ratio, but

Table 3.3 Hedge Ratio Alternatives

Ratio	Equation
Equal-dollar match	$h = -1$
Minimum variance	$h = -\rho_{SF}\sigma_{\Delta S}/\sigma_{\Delta F}$
Statistical estimation	$h =$ Negative of the slope coefficient of regression of ΔF on ΔS
Theoretical	$h = -\Delta S/\Delta F$

it must be formulated carefully to avoid some inaccuracies. The future's pricing relationships can be used as an alternative to calculate the theoretical price movement between the futures contract and the underlying security price in an effort to estimate a minimum-variance hedge ratio.

The Minimum-Variance Hedge Ratio

The hedge ratio needed to minimize the residual risk in the hedge can be related to the generalized hedging framework. The equation, $\Delta V = \Delta S + h\Delta F$, gives the change in the value of the hedged portfolio. The variance of the change in the value of the portfolio is determined by taking the variance of each side of that equation. This step gives the variance of the change in the value of the portfolio as

$$\sigma_{\Delta V}^2 = \sigma_{\Delta S}^2 + h^2\sigma_{\Delta F}^2 + 2h\rho_{SF}\sigma_{\Delta S}\sigma_{\Delta F},$$

where ρ_{SF} is the correlation coefficient between the change in the underlying security price and the futures price. The minimum variance is achieved if h is set equal to

$$\frac{-\rho_{SF}\sigma_{\Delta S}}{\sigma_{\Delta F}},$$

leaving the variance of the hedged portfolio equal to

$$\sigma_{\Delta V}^2 = \sigma_{\Delta S}^2(1 - \rho_{SF}^2).$$

If the price movements between the underlying security and the futures contract used in the hedge are perfectly correlated, the variance of the hedge is equal to zero, indicating that the risk in the underlying security can be completely hedged. Otherwise, the hedge is left with some amount of residual risk. This residual risk is risk in the basis. The hedge converts the full price risk of the security into basis risk or tracking error between the security and the futures contract. The basis risk is usually much smaller than the original price risk the investor faced.

If the change in the futures price is perfectly correlated with the underlying security and matches its variance, the minimum-variance hedge ratio is equal to -1. This ratio would give a result similar to that of the simple hedging framework developed earlier. The investor would match the value of the underlying security to be hedged with

an equal value of futures contracts to create the hedge. In more complicated cases, when the futures price and the underlying security price might not be perfectly correlated or might not have the same volatility, the investor needs to use a hedge ratio different from -1.

Table 3.4 illustrates the minimum-variance hedge ratio for different levels of correlation between the futures price and the underlying security price. If the price changes are perfectly correlated and have the same volatility, the minimum-variance hedge ratio would be equal to -1 and the variance of the hedged portfolio would be completely eliminated. A correlation coefficient of 0.5 would result in a hedge ratio of -0.5 and the portfolio variance would be reduced to 75 percent of the variance of the underlying security itself.

The minimum-variance hedge ratio is sometimes estimated statistically by regressing the change in the futures price on the change in the underlying security price. The negative of the slope coefficient from the regression produces an estimate of the minimum-variance hedge ratio, as illustrated in Figure 3.6. Although this technique is often used to estimate the appropriate hedge ratio, some care must be taken in interpreting the results. Because the regression is usually done using time-series data for successive days or weeks, the regression generally does not accurately account for the natural convergence in the futures price. Changes in a future's price when the future is close to expiration generally have a smaller variance than when it is farther away from expiration. As a result, the typical regression,

Table 3.4 The Minimum-Variance Hedge Ratio: Example

Correlation (ρ_{SF})	Minimum-Variance Hedge Ratio (h)[a]	Ratio of Hedged to Spot Variance $(1 - \rho_{SF}^2)$
1.00	−1.00	0.00
0.95	−0.95	0.10
0.90	−0.90	0.19
0.85	−0.85	0.28
0.80	−0.85	0.36
0.70	−0.70	0.51
0.60	−0.60	0.64
0.50	−0.50	0.75

[a]Assumes that $\sigma_{\Delta S} = \sigma_{\Delta f}$.

Figure 3.6 Statistical Estimation of Hedge Ratios

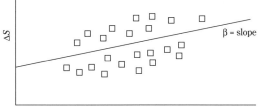

Estimating regression:

$\Delta S = \alpha + \beta\Delta F + \text{Residual error.}$

Hedge ratio:

$h = -\beta$

$= \dfrac{-\rho_{SF}\sigma_{\Delta S}}{\sigma_{\Delta F}}$

which uses futures price data over time, will calculate a hedge ratio that essentially averages the futures price variance over the life of the contract. For many applications, the distortion may be small and may not be important, but for some applications, such as arbitrage (when precision is important in creating the hedge), the statistical procedure may be slightly inaccurate.

Theoretical Hedge Ratios

The arbitrage relationship between the futures contract and the underlying security links the two prices together. This relationship can be used to calculate how the fair price of the futures contract will change as the price of the underlying security changes. To see how this relationship can be used to estimate the minimum-variance hedge ratio, suppose that the price change of both the security to be hedged and the futures contract are proportional to the change in a common index I in the following way:

$\Delta S = c_s\Delta I$, and

$\Delta F = c_f\Delta I,$

where c_s and c_f are the constants of proportionality for the security to be hedged and for the futures contract, respectively.

Because both are tied to the same underlying index, the correlation coefficient between the two is equal to 1.0 and the minimum-variance hedge

ratio is proportional to the ratio of their respective constants. That is,

$$h = \dfrac{-\rho_{SF}\sigma_{\Delta s}}{\sigma_{\Delta F}}$$

$$= \dfrac{-c_s\sigma_{\Delta I}}{c_f\sigma_{\Delta I}}$$

$$= \dfrac{-c_s}{c_f}$$

$$= \dfrac{-\Delta S}{\Delta F}.$$

If the investor has a measure of how the prices of the futures contract and the hedged security change relative to the price of the common index, the investor can calculate the appropriate hedge ratio.

Equity Hedges. Suppose the price of an equity portfolio changes by a factor of beta relative to the market index used by the futures contract. The change in the unit value of the portfolio is given by

$$\Delta S = \beta\Delta I,$$

and the price change in the futures contract with t days to maturity is given by

$$\Delta F = \left(1 + \dfrac{rt}{360}\right)\Delta I,$$

where ΔI is the change in the market index.

The hedge ratio for an equity portfolio can then be calculated as

$$h = \dfrac{-\Delta S}{\Delta F}$$

$$= \dfrac{-\beta}{\left(1 + \dfrac{rt}{360}\right)}.$$

As an example, consider the calculation of the minimum-variance hedge ratio and the number of futures contracts required to hedge a $21 million equity portfolio with a beta of 1.0 relative to the S&P 500 Index. If the futures contract has 35 days to expiration (t), an interest rate (r) of 8.6 percent, and the index stands at 330, the hedge ratio is

$$h = \frac{-1.0}{\left[1 + \left(\dfrac{0.086 \times 35}{360}\right)\right]} = -0.99.$$

The contract size for the S&P 500 is 500 times the value of the S&P 500 Index, or $165,000, so the number of futures contracts required to be sold is

$$n = \frac{h(\text{Hedge value})}{\text{Contract size}} = \frac{-0.99(21,000,000)}{165,000}$$

$$= -126.2 \text{ contracts.}$$

Notice that with the futures contract's expiration date beyond the short-term investment horizon of the hedge, the hedge ratio is not an equal-dollar match even with the beta of the equity portfolio equal to 1. The reason is that the variance of the price movement of the futures contract before expiration is slightly larger than the variance of the price movement of the index itself because of incomplete convergence before expiration in the price of the futures contract.[6]

Foreign Exchange Hedges. For a foreign exchange contract, the change in the futures contract's price relative to the change in the spot exchange rate is equal to

$$\Delta F = \frac{\Delta S \left(1 + \dfrac{r_d t}{360}\right)}{\left(1 + \dfrac{r_f t}{360}\right)},$$

and the hedge ratio is

$$h = \frac{-\left(1 + \dfrac{r_f t}{360}\right)}{\left(1 + \dfrac{r_d t}{360}\right)},$$

where t represents the days to maturity of the futures contract.

As an example of how to hedge foreign exchange exposure, consider a hedge against a 10

billion yen exposure in which the futures contract expires in 42 days (t), the U.S. interest rate (r_d) is 8.5 percent, and the Japanese interest rate (r_f) is 10.3 percent. The contract size is 12.5 million yen. The hedge ratio is

$$h = \frac{-\left(1 + \dfrac{r_f t}{360}\right)}{\left(1 + \dfrac{r_d t}{360}\right)} = \frac{-\left(1 + \dfrac{[0.103(42)]}{360}\right)}{\left(1 + \dfrac{[0.085(42)]}{360}\right)}$$

$$= -1.002,$$

and the number of contracts required is

$$n = \frac{h \text{ (Hedge value)}}{\text{Contract size}} = \frac{[-1.002(10,000,000,000\,)]}{12,500,000}$$

$$= -801.6.$$

Because the hedge ratio is -1.002, 802 contracts need to be sold to hedge the 10 billion yen exposure. In this case, the relative interest rates are close enough that the short-term hedge ratio is essentially an equal-dollar match.

Interest Rate Hedges. Figure 3.7 shows the most popular futures contracts used in hedging interest rates along the term-structure curve. Short-term rates tend to fluctuate more widely than longer term rates, and Treasury bill futures and Eurodollar futures are useful to hedge short-term rate fluctuations. The Treasury note futures have a somewhat longer maturity, and the Treasury bond futures are positioned at the long end of the curve. The hedge ratios are calculated in

Figure 3.7   Futures for Interest Rate Hedging

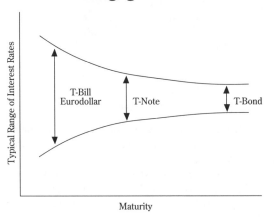

---

[6]Arbitrage conditions for a perfectly matched hedge held until expiration would indicate that the hedge ratio should be 1.0 requiring 127.3 contracts to be sold. Slightly fewer contracts are needed for a very short-term hedge because of the slightly higher price movement in the futures contract caused by its pricing relative to the index.

exactly the same manner for the Treasury bonds and notes, but there are some differences for the Treasury bill and Eurodollar futures.

Treasury Bill Hedges. The change in the price per dollar face value of a Treasury bill with t days to maturity is equal to

$$\Delta S = -\left(\frac{t}{360}\right)\Delta d,$$

where Δd is the change in the discount rate on the Treasury bill. The change in the price of the futures contract per dollar face value is equal to

$$\Delta F = 0.25\Delta d_f,$$

where Δd_f is the change in the discount rate on the futures contract. Consequently, the hedge ratio is

$$h = \frac{-\left(\dfrac{t}{360}\right)}{0.25}\left(\frac{\Delta d}{\Delta d_f}\right),$$

where $(\Delta d/\Delta d_f)$ represents the movement in the discount rate for the underlying Treasury bill relative to the futures discount rate. This ratio would typically be 1 for parallel moves in the yield curve.

As an example of hedging a Treasury bill, consider a $20 million exposure with 20 days to maturity. The ratio of Δd to Δd_f is assumed to be 1.0, and the contract size is $1 million. The hedge ratio is

$$h = \frac{-\left(\dfrac{20}{360}\right)}{0.25}(1.0) = -0.22.$$

The number of contracts required is

$$n = \frac{h\ (\text{Hedge value})}{\text{Contract size}} = \frac{-0.22(20,000,000)}{1,000,000}$$

$$= -4.4.$$

With a hedge ratio of -0.22, about four futures contracts have to be sold to hedge the exposure. Only a small number of contracts is needed because each contract represents the interest exposure for 90 days on a $1 million Treasury bill. The bill to be hedged has only 20 days of interest exposure left, so each contract can hedge the interest exposure of more than $4 million of principal.

Eurodollar Hedges. For a security such as a Eurodollar deposit paying a fixed interest rate, the change in the price of the security per dollar of principal from a change in the market yield of the security is equal to

$$\Delta S = \frac{-\left(\dfrac{t}{360}\right)\Delta r}{\left(1 + \dfrac{rt}{360}\right)}.$$

The change in the price of a Eurodollar future per dollar of face value is equal to

$$\Delta F = -0.25\Delta r_f,$$

where Δr_f represents the change in the futures interest rate. Thus, the hedge ratio is

$$h = \frac{-\left(\dfrac{t}{360}\right)}{0.25\left(1 + \dfrac{rt}{360}\right)}\left(\frac{\Delta r}{\Delta r_f}\right),$$

where $(\Delta r/\Delta r_f)$ is the relative movement in interest rates between the security being hedged and the Eurodollar futures contract.

The example below illustrates the calculation of the hedge ratio for a $40 million position in securities that has 45 days left before maturity with a current yield of 8.83 percent. The relative movement in the interest rates on the security and the Eurodollar futures $(\Delta r/\Delta r_f)$ is assumed to be 1.0, and the contract size is $1 million. The hedge ratio is equal to

$$h = \frac{-\left(\dfrac{45}{360}\right)}{0.25\left(1 + \dfrac{0.0883(45)}{360}\right)}(1) = -0.49,$$

and the number of contracts required is

$$n = \frac{-0.49(40,000,000)}{1,000,000} = -19.6 \text{ contracts.}$$

The hedge position requires only half as many contracts as an equal-dollar-matched position because the securities have only 45 days of interest exposure left, but the futures contract embodies 90 days of interest exposure. Each contract can cover approximately twice the interest exposure per dollar face value of the security position.

Treasury Note and Bond Hedges. The change in the value of a note or bond from a change in its yield to maturity has the following relationship to the duration of the security:

$$\Delta B = -D^*B\Delta y_B,$$

where B is the security price, D^* is the modified duration of the security, and y_B is the security's yield to maturity. The change in the value of the Treasury note or bond futures contract is equal to

$$\Delta F = -D_F^*F\Delta y,$$

where F represents the futures price, D_F is the modified duration of the futures contract, and y is the yield to maturity of the cheapest-to-deliver (CTD) note or bond.

A review of duration and its relationship to a change in the price of a fixed-income security is given in Appendix C. Using the concept of duration to measure interest rate risk allows us to write the hedge ratio as

$$h = \frac{-D^*B}{D_F^*F}\left(\frac{\Delta y_B}{\Delta y}\right).$$

To illustrate the calculation of the hedge ratio, consider a $28 million bond position hedged with Treasury bond futures contracts. The security price is 94²⁄₃₂ (94.0625), the futures price is 93¹⁶⁄₃₂ (93.50), and the modified durations of the security and the futures contract are 10.3 years and 9.4 years, respectively. The ratio of the change in yield to maturity of the security to that of the CTD note or bond ($\Delta y_B/\Delta y$) is assumed to be 0.95, and the CTD contract size is $92,500. The hedge ratio is

$$h = \frac{-10.3(94.0625)}{9.4(93.50)}(0.95) = -1.05,$$

which would require that approximately 318 futures contracts be sold to hedge the $28 million position in underlying securities:

$$n = \frac{-1.05(28,000,000)}{92,500} = -317.8 \text{ contracts.}$$

Controlling Asset Exposure: Asset Allocation

Recall that the change in the value of a portfolio resulting from holding an underlying asset position and h futures contracts would be

$$\Delta V = \Delta S + h\Delta F.$$

This basic relationship can be used to suggest how futures contracts can be used to alter the mix of stocks, bonds, and cash in a portfolio.

Suppose an investor wants the investment value to change as if θ_V^E proportion of the portfolio were invested in equity with β_v sensitivity to the market index. Suppose also that the current portfolio of underlying assets has θ_s proportion invested in equity with β_s sensitivity to the market index. The desired change in portfolio value as a result of its equity exposure is

$$\theta_V^E\beta_V\Delta I = \theta_S\beta_S\Delta I + h_E\left(1 + \frac{rt}{360}\right)\Delta I.$$

Solving for the equity hedge ratio required to produce the desired effect gives

$$h_E = \frac{\theta_V^E\beta_V - \theta_S\beta_S}{\left(1 + \dfrac{rt}{360}\right)}.$$

In addition, suppose the investor wants the portfolio to change as if θ_V^B proportion is invested in bonds with modified duration D_V^* while the portfolio of underlying assets has θ_B proportion invested in bonds with modified duration D_B^*. We can write the desired change in portfolio value because of its bond exposure as

$$-\theta_V^BD_V^*B\Delta y_B = -\theta_BD_B^*B\Delta y_B - h_BD_F^*F\Delta y.$$

Solving for the bond hedge ratio required to produce the desired effect gives

$$h_B = \frac{B(\theta_V^BD_V^* - \theta_BD_B^*)}{D_F^*F}\left(\frac{\Delta y_B}{\Delta y}\right).$$

The two hedging equations allow the investor to calculate—given the current composition and risk exposure in the underlying portfolio—the appropriate hedge ratios to use in creating the desired equity and bond exposure in the portfolio. The calculation of the required number of futures contracts is basically an issue of scale. The number of futures contracts is equal to the hedge ratio times the size of the portfolio position to be altered divided by the unit value of each futures contract. The contract unit value reflects the value of the underlying asset covered by the futures contract.

For example, suppose an investor has a portfolio of $20 million with the current and desired characteristics shown below.

Characteristic	Desired Exposure (V)	Underlying Asset Exposure
θ (Stocks)	0.60	0.50
θ (Bonds)	0.40	0.50
β	1.00	0.93
D*	10.00	9.50

Assume also that the Treasury bond futures contract has a modified duration of 10.03 with the futures priced at $98^{16}/_{32}$. The price of the underlying CTD bond is $99^{16}/_{32}$, giving a contract value of $99,500 per contract, and the price of the bonds in the underlying portfolio is equal to $99^{8}/_{32}$. Furthermore, assume that the relative yield movement between the bonds in the portfolio and the CTD Treasury bond is 1.0. The futures contracts expire in 35 days, the current short-term interest rate is 7.3 percent for that period, and the S&P 500 Index is priced at 330.00, giving a value of $165,000 per contract.

The hedge ratio for the desired equity exposure is equal to

$$h_E = \frac{\theta_V^E \beta_V - \theta_S \beta_S}{\left(1 + \frac{rt}{360}\right)}$$

$$= \frac{0.60(1.0) - 0.50(0.93)}{1 + \frac{0.073(35)}{360}}$$

$$= 0.13,$$

and the number of futures contracts required to achieve this exposure is

$$n_E = \frac{h_E \theta_V^E \,(\text{Portfolio value})}{\text{Contract size}}$$

$$= \frac{0.13(0.60)\,(20,000,000)}{165,000}$$

$$= 9.5 \text{ contracts.}$$

The hedge ratio for the desired bond exposure is equal to

$$h_B = \frac{B(\theta_V^B D_V^* - \theta_B D_B^*)}{D_F^* F}\left(\frac{\Delta y_B}{\Delta y}\right)$$

$$= \frac{99.25[0.40(10.0) - 0.50(9.5)]}{10.03(98.5)}(1.0)$$

$$= -0.08,$$

and the number of futures contracts required to achieve this exposure is

$$n_B = \frac{h_B \theta_V^B \,(\text{Portfolio value})}{\text{CTD Contract size}}$$

$$= \frac{-0.08(0.40)(20,000,000)}{99,500}$$

$$= -6.4 \text{ contracts.}$$

The principles involved in the asset-exposure decision are not really any different from the hedging principles developed earlier in this chapter. The goal is to determine the appropriate number of futures contracts required to produce a specific level of exposure to underlying price risk. Once the hedge is set, the portfolio, with its futures contracts, behaves as if the underlying assets had been adjusted to reflect the desired level of risk in the underlying portfolio exposure.

Delta-neutral or complete hedging tries to eliminate the full price risk. Synthetic asset creation adds or subtracts risk exposure to an investment position. They are two sides of the same process, with all of the possible degrees in between. Once investors understand how the futures contract moves relative to the underlying asset, they can tailor the level of exposure to meet their objectives and preferences in either a moderate or aggressive manner.

4. Option Characteristics and Strategies: Risk and Return

The two basic types of options are a *call* option and a *put* option. The call option gives a person the right to buy a security at a specified price within a specified period of time (see Figure 4.1). For example, a call option on the S&P 500 gives an investor the right to buy units of the S&P 500 Index at a set price within a specified amount of time. In contrast, the put option gives the investor the right to sell a security at a specified price within a particular period of time. An investor may buy a call or put option and may also sell a call or put option. Keeping track of how each option behaves can sometimes be confusing, but understanding how put and call options behave differently, depending on whether they are bought or sold, can reduce the confusion in analyzing complex strategies.

Option Characteristics

Options have several important characteristics. One is the *strike* or *exercise price*. This price gives

Figure 4.1   Options

	Call	Put
Buy	Right to Buy the Security	Right to Sell the Security
Sell	May Have to Sell the Security	May Have to Buy the Security

the value at which the investor can purchase the underlying security. The *maturity* of the option defines the time period within which the investor can buy or sell the security at the exercise price.

Three terms—*at the money, in the money,* and *out of the money*—identify where the current security price is relative to the strike or exercise price. For example, a call option that has a strike price of $100 when the security price is $120 is in the money, because the investor can buy the security for less than its market price. Similarly, a put option with a strike price of $100 while the security is priced at $90 would be in the money because the investor can sell the security for more than its market price.

Some options can be exercised early, but some can only be exercised on the specific maturity date. An option that can be exercised early is called an *American* option; an option that can be exercised only at the maturity date is a *European* option. Most of the options traded on organized exchanges are American options, although a few European option contracts are traded, as well.

An option with a strike or exercise price that is adjusted for any dividends or interest paid on the underlying security is called *payout protected*. Most exchange-traded options are not payout protected.

Analysts have come to think of the option price or premium as being composed of two parts—the

Figure 4.2 Option Price

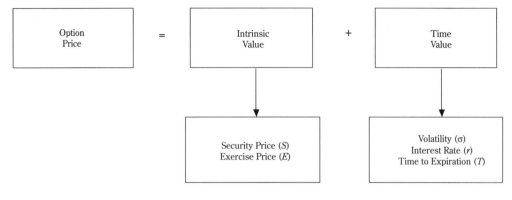

Call Intrinsic Value = max(0, S - E)
Put Intrinsic Value = max(0, E - S)

intrinsic value and the *time value*—as illustrated in Figure 4.2. The intrinsic value is the amount of money that would be received if an investor were to purchase the security at the exercise price and immediately sell it for the current market price. The intrinsic value depends on the relationship between the security price and the exercise price of the option. The intrinsic value of a call option is the maximum of either zero or the difference between the security price and the exercise price $(S - E)$. If $S - E$ is positive, the call option is in the money and has a positive intrinsic value. If $S - E$ is negative, the call option is out of the money and has zero intrinsic value. The intrinsic value of a put option is just the reverse: the maximum of zero or $E - S$. If $E - S$ is positive, the put option is in the money. If $E - S$ is negative, the put option is out of the money and has zero intrinsic value.

The *time value* of an option is a function of the security's volatility, or risk (σ); the current level of interest rates (r); and the option's maturity, or time to expiration (T). The difference between the option price and intrinsic value is the time value. The option's positive time value gradually approaches zero at expiration, with the option price at expiration equal to its intrinsic value. The option price's convergence to its intrinsic value at expiration is similar to the convergence of a futures contract to the underlying security price at expiration.

Some hypothetical option prices will illustrate these concepts: Consider the IBM call options presented in Table 4.1. On January 8, 1991, IBM

closed at a price of $119½. The table lists options with three different strike prices at three different maturities. These prices illustrate several important properties of option prices.

- A call option that is in the money should be worth at least as much as its intrinsic value. Notice that the $110 call is in the money and its intrinsic value is $9½. Each $110 call option should be worth at least $9½.
- Call options having the same strike price but with longer maturities are more valuable than those with shorter maturities because the stock has more time in which to rise above the strike price; that is, the time value increases with maturity. Note that the price of the $110 call option rises from $9⅞ to $15 as the maturity increases.
- Call options having the same maturity but with higher strike prices are more out of the money and, therefore, are worth less because a larger (but less likely) move in the stock price will be needed for the option to pay off. Notice that the price of the

Table 4.1 IBM Call Options, January 8, 1991

		Expiration Month		
Close	Strike	Jan.	Apr.	July
$119½	$110	$9⅞	$12½	$15
119½	120	1⅝	5⅜	8½
119½	130	1/16	2	4

January call option falls from $9⅞ to $¹⁄₁₆ as the strike price increases.

The value of a call option with its intrinsic value and time value is illustrated in Figure 4.3. Notice that the call price increases as the security value increases. Also, the time value reaches a maximum at the exercise price and then declines toward zero as the option goes in the money.

Figure 4.3   Value of a Call Option

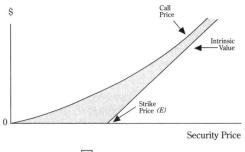

Time Value

Put options behave in much the same fashion as call options and possess similar properties, as illustrated in Table 4.2.

- A put option that is in the money should be worth at least as much as its intrinsic value. Note that the intrinsic value of the $120 put is $½; each of the $120 put options should be worth at least that much.
- Put options having the same strike price but with longer maturities are more valuable than those with shorter maturities. Notice that the price of the $120 put increases from $1¾ to $5⅛ as the maturity increases.
- Put options having the same maturity but with lower strike prices are more out of the

Table 4.2   IBM Put Options, January 8, 1991

| Close | Strike | Expiration Month | | |
		Jan.	Apr.	July
$119½	$110	$ ¹⁄₁₆	$ 1⅛	$ 2³⁄₁₆
119½	120	1¾	4⅛	5⅛
119½	130	10½	11⅜	11¾

money and, therefore, worth less. The price of the January put declines from $10½ to $¹⁄₁₆ as the strike price declines.

Figure 4.4 illustrates the conceptual value of a put option, its intrinsic value, and its time value. These option-pricing relationships for both the put and the call are summarized as follows:

	Call Option	Put Option
Exercise price	$C(E_1) \geq C(E_2)$	$P(E_1) \leq P(E_2)$
Time to expiration	$C(t_1) \leq C(t_2)$	$P(t_1) \leq P(t_2)$
Intrinsic value	$C \geq \max(0, S_0 - E)$	$P \geq \max(0, E - S_0)$

where

E	= exercise price,
S_0	= current price of security,
P	= put option price,
C	= call option price,
$t_1 < t_2$	= expiration relationship, and
$E_1 < E_2$	= strike price relationship.

Figure 4.4   Value of a Put Option

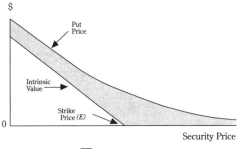

Time Value

One other property of options should be noted. An option can move in a very leveraged way relative to the underlying security. The leverage in an option is part of what makes it useful for controlling risk, but its price can be extremely volatile when the option is held by itself. Table 4.3 illustrates the leverage capability of an option. In this simple example, a call option with a strike price of $60 is assumed. The security price increases in increments from $50 to $80, which increases the intrinsic value of the option. The time value of the option first increases, then decreases as the security and option prices increase. Notice, however, the percentage changes in the stock and option prices. The security has

31

Table 4.3 Options and Leverage

Item	Security Price			
	$50	$60[a]	$70	$80
Intrinsic value of call option	$0.0	$0.0	$10.0	$20.0
Time value of option	2.0	3.0	2.0	1.0
Total option premium	2.0	3.0	12.0	21.0
Change in security price	—	20.0%	16.7%	14.3%
Change in option price	—	50.0	300.0	75.0

[a]Exercise price of the call option.

Figure 4.5 Payoff Profile of a Call Option

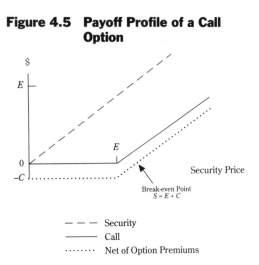

---- Security
——— Call
········ Net of Option Premiums

relatively modest increases in price, but the option has large percentage changes once it is in the money. The dollar price changes are similar between the stock and the option once it goes in the money, but the percentage price changes are much higher for the lower priced option.

Payoff Profiles. Insight into the characteristics of options can be obtained by looking specifically at how options behave and what value they have at expiration. The matrix below is a simple technique for showing the value of option positions:

	$S < E$	$S > E$
Call	0	$S - E$
Put	$E - S$	0
Security	S	S

At the expiration of the put or call option, its intrinsic value depends on whether the security price is less than the exercise price or more than the exercise price. The value of the underlying security is the same, S, whether it is below or above the option's exercise price. These concepts are the basic building blocks for option strategy analysis.

Figure 4.5 illustrates the payoff pattern at expiration for a call option. On the horizontal axis is plotted the security price. The vertical axis measures the value of the underlying security and the net payoff. The trivial case representing the security's value is shown by the dashed line. For example, if the security ends with a value of E dollars, then the security will have a payoff of E dollars. The call option has a value of zero until the security price reaches the exercise price E, after

which the call option increases one for one in price as the security price increases. The investor, however, must purchase the option initially. So the net payoff from buying a call option is negative until the security price reaches the exercise price, and then it starts to rise (the dotted line). This line represents the payoff the investor receives net of the cost of the option. The investor breaks even with zero net profit at the point where the security price equals the strike price plus the call option premium.

Note that the call option has a kinked or asymmetric payoff pattern. This feature distinguishes it from a futures contract. The future has a payoff pattern that is a straight line, as does the underlying security. This payoff asymmetry allows the option to create specialized return patterns that are unavailable when using a futures contract.

Figure 4.6 illustrates the behavior of a put option. The put option has an intrinsic value of zero above the exercise price. From there, it increases one for one as the security price declines. If an investor buys a put option, the net payoff of the option is the dotted line. The investor breaks even, with zero net profit, at the point where the security price equals the strike price less the put option premium.

Option Strategies

These payoff profiles allow examination of some common option strategies. These strategies include the covered call, protective put, straddle, and the bull call spread.

Figure 4.6 Payoff Profile of a Put Option

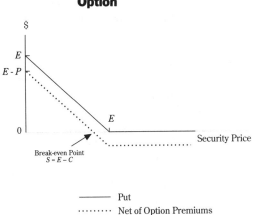

————— Put

········· Net of Option Premiums

Figure 4.7 Payoff Profile of a Covered Call

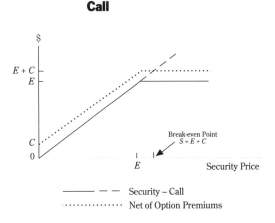

— — — Security – Call

············· Net of Option Premiums

Covered Call. An investor constructs a covered-call position by buying the underlying security and selling a call option. The value matrix shown below can be used to see how this investment strategy behaves.

	$S < E$	$S > E$
Security	S	S
−Call	0	$-(S - E)$
Total payoff	S	E

The security has a value of S whether it is above or below the option's exercise price. The call option has a value of zero below the exercise price. Above the exercise price, the call option has a value of $S - E$. Because the call option has been sold instead of purchased, however, the payoff requires a negative sign. Totaling up the columns shows what the payoff is when the security is above and below the exercise price at expiration. When the security price is below the exercise price, the investment is worth S dollars. When the security price is above the exercise price, the investment is worth E dollars.

The dashed line in Figure 4.7 illustrates the payoff for the security. The covered-call portfolio is worth S dollars until the security reaches a price of E. Above E dollars, the portfolio is worth only E dollars. The solid line represents the value of the portfolio based on the final value of the security price. The dotted line represents the total covered-call value when the option premium that has been received by selling the call option is taken into account.

The benefit of this strategy occurs below the exercise price, where the investment is always worth a little bit more than the security. The risk of the strategy lies above the strike price: If the security price rises too much, the portfolio will not participate in the market rise. As a result, this strategy works well when the security price is stable or going down but not well when the price goes up a lot. The break-even point occurs when the security price equals the strike price plus the original price of the call option. Below this point, the covered-call strategy gives a better payoff than just holding the security itself.

Protective Put. A protective put is constructed by holding the underlying security and buying a put option. The value matrix for this strategy is

	$S < E$	$S > E$
Security	S	S
Put	$E - S$	0
Total payoff	E	S

The value of the security is S whether it moves above or below the exercise price. The value of the put option is $E - S$ below the option's exercise price and zero above the exercise price. The total value of the protective put is found by adding up the value in each column. Below the exercise price, the portfolio is worth E dollars at expiration. Above the exercise price, it is worth S.

This strategy is depicted graphically in Figure 4.8. The dashed line again represents the security

Figure 4.8 Payoff Profile of a Protective Put

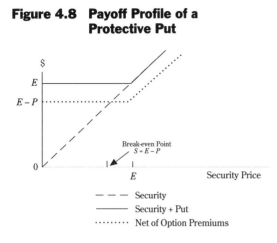

- - - Security
——— Security + Put
········· Net of Option Premiums

value. The solid line represents the value of the security plus the put option. Below the exercise price, the put option compensates for the decline in the security price. Once the original cost of the put option is accounted for, the net payoff is represented by the dotted line. The break-even point occurs when the security price is equal to the strike price less the cost of the put option. Below this point, the protective-put strategy gives a better payoff than just holding the security itself.

The benefit of this strategy occurs below the exercise price. At this level, the portfolio is always worth more than the security itself. This protection is of great benefit if the market is going down. The market does not give this protection for free, however. Above the exercise price, the protected portfolio is always worth a little bit less than the security. The price paid for the option results in a slightly lower return on the upside. This strategy has sometimes taken on another name, *portfolio insurance*, because the put option protects the value if the security price falls while maintaining some market exposure if the price rises.

Straddle. The straddle is a strategy that involves the purchase of both a put option and a call option but does not involve the purchase of the security itself. The value matrix for this strategy is

	$S < E$	$S > E$
Call	0	$S - E$
Put	$E - S$	0
Total payoff	$E - S$	$S - E$

The call option has a value of zero below E and a value of $S - E$ above E. The put option has a value of $E - S$ below E and a value of zero above E. The total payoff is $E - S$ below E and $S - E$ above E.

In Figure 4.9, the net payoff for the strategy is illustrated by the dotted line. The break-even points for this strategy are on each side of the strike price. The investor shows positive profits if the security price falls outside either break-even point. The investor makes money so long as the security price moves away from the strike price. If the security price moves up, the investor makes money; if the security price moves down, the investor makes money; but, if the price stays relatively constant, the investor loses money. This strategy is useful when the investor is very uncertain about the direction of a price change but is fairly confident that some price change will occur.

Figure 4.9 Payoff Profile of a Straddle

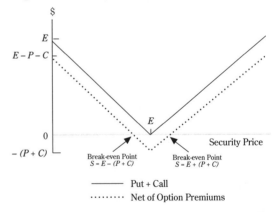

——— Put + Call
········· Net of Option Premiums

Bull Call Spread. The bull call spread is a somewhat more complex strategy than those previously discussed. It involves options at more than one strike price. Because the investor needs to know how the option will behave both above and below each strike price, the value matrix must be enlarged into three pieces. The bull call spread is constructed by buying a call option with an exercise price of E_1 and selling a call option with an exercise price of E_2. The strike price E_2 is larger than the strike price E_1. The value matrix for this strategy is

	$S < E_1$	$E_1 < S < E_2$	$S > E_2$
Call (E_1)	0	$S - E_1$	$S - E_1$
$-$Call (E_2)	0	0	$-(S - E_2)$
Total payoff	0	$S - E_1$	$E_2 - E_1$

Consider the first call option and its value. Below its strike price E_1, this call option has no value. So long as S is greater than E_1, this call option is in the money and has a value of $S - E_1$. The value of this call option does not depend on E_2, only on E_1.

The second call option has an exercise price of E_2. It has no value as long as the security price is less than E_2. When the security price is greater than E_2, its value is $-(S - E_2)$. The minus sign in front indicates this option has been sold. The total payoff at expiration is zero when the security price is below E_1, $S - E_1$ when the security price is between E_1 and E_2, and $E_2 - E_1$ above E_2.

The result is illustrated graphically in Figure 4.10. Until the security price reaches E_1, the investment has a value of zero. Above the value of E_2, the investment has a value of $E_2 - E_1$. Between E_2 and E_1, the value is just a straight line connecting the two. Once the net value of the option premiums is accounted for, the dotted line results. The break-even point for this strategy occurs when the security price equals the lower strike price E_1 plus the net cost of the two call options. This strategy offers highly controlled risk. Loss is limited if the security price declines, but the gain is also limited if the security price goes up. It is called a bull call spread because it is constructed using call options and reflects the investor's bullish sentiment on the security. The maximum benefit occurs if the price goes up moderately, but the loss is limited if the investor is wrong and the security price declines.

Pre-Expiration Strategies. The examples to this point illustrate a technique for analyzing the payoff pattern from an option strategy. Although this technique is simple, it is also important. Option strategies can become very complex, and keeping track of all of the pieces at once is often difficult. Value matrixes and their associated payoff profiles allow the investor to combine all the pieces to describe the net result of a strategy if it is held to expiration. This technique offers an investor insight into what is happening when options are used in an investment strategy.

Many option strategies, however, are not held to expiration of the options. In this case, the payoff patterns maintain a similar shape, but the kinked payoff segments are usually smoothed into gradual curves. For example, Figure 4.11 illustrates the profit profile of the bull call spread before expiration. Note that the sharp edges of the profile in Figure 4.10 at expiration are smoothed in Figure 4.11. As the time to expiration draws near, the profile becomes sharper and draws close to the expiration shape. Drawing payoff patterns without holding the options to expiration, however, requires the use of an option-pricing model to value the option positions.

Figure 4.11 Payoff Profile of a Bull Call Spread Before Expiration

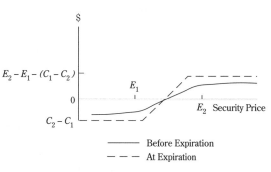

— Before Expiration
‒ ‒ ‒ At Expiration

Choosing a Strategy

Figure 4.12 represents two basic considerations the investor must deal with when formulating an option strategy. The two general parame-

Figure 4.10 Payoff Profile of a Bull Call Spread

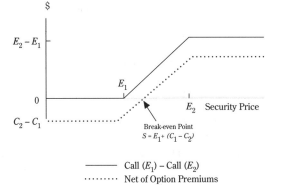

—— Call (E_1) – Call (E_2)
········· Net of Option Premiums

ters relate to market direction and the cost of the options. First, in general, when an investor is bullish, the best strategies involve buying call options or selling put options. When bearish, the best strategies involve buying puts or selling calls. When neutral, the investor often wants to sell options instead of purchasing them so as to capture the time value of the option premium.

Figure 4.12   Option Strategies: Market Direction vs. Option Price

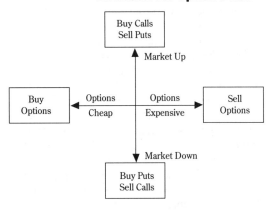

The second dimension relates to the cost of the options. If the options are considered expensive, an investor generally does better selling those options than buying them. If the options are considered cheap, the investor generally does better purchasing options. Thus, an expectation of market direction and an assessment of the expensiveness of option prices help the investor establish a broad framework within which to develop option strategies. For example, if the investor is bearish and options are not expensive, buying put options outright or using a protected-put strategy with the underlying security is attractive. If the investor is neutral in market outlook and options are expensive, a covered-call strategy or selling a straddle (selling both a put and a call) is attractive. The choice of strike prices on the options and their maturities create additional flexibility for the investor, but the most important considerations generally relate to a view of market direction and option cost.

At this point, the discussion has not dealt with the bases for judging whether option prices are cheap or expensive. When options are considered to be expensive, most investors refer to them as

having higher-than-normal volatility; cheap options are said to have lower-than-normal volatility. The introduction of option-pricing models in Chapter 5 will show how option prices depend on the risk or volatility of the underlying security.

Probability Distribution of Returns

In addition to using payoff diagrams to describe the effect of options, an investor can look at the probability distribution of returns for various strategies. Consider first the covered-call strategy. Figure 4.13 shows probability distributions of returns for an underlying security with and without use of call options. Note how the shape changes as an increasing proportion of call options are sold relative to the underlying security position. Selling call options draws the portfolio distribution back gradually on the right side and increases the chance that an investor will receive only moderate returns. Selling call options on 100 percent of the portfolio completely truncates the right-hand side of the probability distribution: The investor has a very high probability of receiving moderate returns and no probability of receiving high returns.

Figure 4.13   Probablility Distribution for a Covered Call

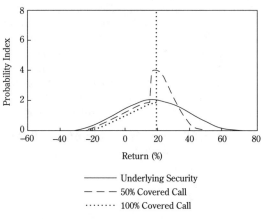

Figure 4.14 illustrates the effect of buying puts on the value of the portfolio. Buying put options truncates the left side of the probability distribution and increases the probability of moderate returns. Most of the probability of high returns is preserved, however.

Figure 4.14 shows the effects of purchasing less than 100 percent of the value of the portfolio in put options. A less aggressive strategy draws

Figure 4.14 Probability Distribution for a Protective Put

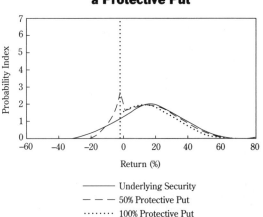

Underlying Security
— — — 50% Protective Put
·········· 100% Protective Put

the left side of the return distribution back moderately while increasing the probability of returns around the exercise price of the option.

Figure 4.15 illustrates the effect of selling call options and buying put options simultaneously. The combination causes quite a severe misshaping of the probability distribution in both tails. The line is no longer smooth and symmetric. The asymmetry of options allows an investor to shape and mold the probability distribution by truncating some parts and adding to others. Call options affect the right tail most dramatically, while put options affect the left tail.

Figure 4.15 Probability Distribution for a Covered Call and Protective Put

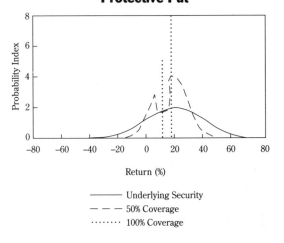

Underlying Security
— — — 50% Coverage
·········· 100% Coverage

Performance Comparisons

Three techniques are sometimes used to compare the returns from different investment alternatives. The first method uses a mean–variance comparison. Table 4.4 shows the mean return, standard deviation, and skewness of a covered-call and a protective-put strategy. Both strategies reduce the mean and standard deviation from that of the underlying security itself, but they do so in different proportions. In this example, the covered-call strategy appears to give more return per unit of risk.

Table 4.4 Mean–Variance Comparison of Option Strategies

Measure	Underlying Stocks	Covered Call[a]	Protective Put[b]
Mean return	15.00%	12.10%	12.90%
Standard deviation	20.00%	10.00%	16.20%
Skewness	0.00	−2.10	0.80
Mean/standard deviation	0.80	1.20	0.80
Average beta	1.00	0.40	0.77

[a]Calls are sold with exercise prices 10 percent out of the money on 100 percent of the portfolio.
[b]Puts are purchased with exercise prices at the money on 100 percent of the portfolio.

Figure 4.16 compares the risk/return relationship of covered calls and protective puts from Table 4.4 by plotting expected return on the vertical axis and standard deviation of returns on the horizontal axis. The center line represents the

Figure 4.16 Risk/Return Trade-Offs for Increasing Option Positions

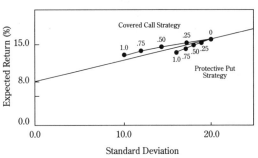

Note: Each point represents a different portion of options used on the portfolio.

common capital market line for equities. Using the covered-call strategy on portions of the portfolio tends to move the portfolio return above the capital market line. Using protective puts tends to move the portfolio return below the capital market line. Selling calls apparently gives better risk-adjusted returns than are available in the market, and buying puts gives poorer risk-adjusted returns. Neither of these portfolios, however, is necessarily more desirable or mispriced. Indeed, the simulated distributions assume that the options are fairly priced and that the market is fully efficient in executing the option strategies.

Once probability distributions are no longer symmetric, judging which portfolio is superior or inferior using mean–variance analysis is difficult. The difficulty lies in the use of standard deviation to capture risk; it no longer tells the whole story. Portfolios with options are much more complex than are those with standard symmetric probability distributions for which standard deviation may serve as an adequate description of risk. Consequently, a comparison of optionlike returns against the capital market line is not reliable for judging the performance of portfolios with options. Optionlike portfolios can be fairly priced while appearing to give superior or inferior risk-adjusted returns. The problem lies in our imperfect measures of risk adjustment for nonsymmetric return distributions.[7]

This same lack of comparability results when using two popular performance measures: the Sharpe ratio and the Treynor ratio, as presented in Table 4.5. Using the data from the covered-call and protective-put strategies indicates that the covered-call position has more attractive ratios than the protective put, even though both strategies use options that are fairly priced. The investor might suspect that something is not quite right in such a comparison, however, because the protective-put strategy reduces much of the undesirable, or downside, risk, while the covered call eliminates the upside gains. The fault, again, lies in applying to very skewed distributions measures that work best for symmetric return distributions. The measures can break down and give false signals.

A second way to compare returns is to examine the probability range of returns. Table 4.6 gives the probabilities of returns falling in various ranges for the covered-call and protective-put strategies in comparison with the probabilities for the underlying security. Notice that the covered-call strategy has a high probability of moderate returns but no probability of large returns. On the other hand, the protective put has no probability of very low returns but preserves some probability of high returns. The return-range technique gives an investor some idea of what trade-offs are being made within each range of returns if options are used. The investor is still left to decide, however, which trade-offs are preferred.

Table 4.5 Portfolio Performance Measures

Strategy	Sharpe Ratio $(\bar{R} - r)/\sigma$	Treynor Ratio $(\bar{R} - r)/\beta$
Stock portfolio	0.35	7.00
Covered call[a]	0.41	10.25
Protective put[b]	0.30	6.36

[a]Calls are sold with exercise prices 10 percent out of the money on 100 percent of the portfolio.
[b]Puts are purchased with exercise prices at the money on 100 percent of the portfolio.

Table 4.6 Comparison of Return Range Probability

Percentage Return Range	Underlying Stock	Covered Call[a]	Protective Put[b]
Below −15	6.7%	2.9%	0.0%
−15 to −5	9.2	5.3	0.0
−5 to 5	15.0	10.4	39.7
5 to 15	19.1	16.1	19.7
15 to 25	19.1	65.3	17.6
25 to 35	15.0	0.0	12.2
Above 35	15.9	0.0	10.8
Total	100.0%	100.0%	100.0%

[a]Calls are sold with exercise prices 10 percent out of the money on 100 percent of the portfolio.
[b]Puts are purchased with exercise prices at the money on 100 percent of the portfolio.

---

[7]See Bookstaber and Clarke (1985) for a discussion of this problem.

A third technique sometimes used to compare probability distributions is called stochastic dominance, a technique that has been known for some time but has only recently been applied to options. Stochastic dominance uses the information from all of the probability distribution, not merely the mean and variance. This approach allows comparison of very skewed distributions and is a natural application for portfolios with options. Unfortunately, the technique is not easy to use and does not always show that one probability distribution is preferable. In fact, if options are fairly priced, the stochastic-dominance technique using simple assumptions of investor risk aversion and preference for positive skewness fails to show that covered calls or protective puts would be preferred over merely holding the underlying security by itself. More has to be known about specific investor preferences before a comparison of option strategies can yield unambiguous results.[8]

In the final analysis, no easy techniques are available that allow an investor to compare two return distributions from option strategies and decide that one strategy is definitely better than another. The use of options can cause such distortions to a standard symmetric return distribution that comparisons are tricky. Particularly susceptible to error are techniques that use only mean and variance measures. Typically, an investor must make trade-offs between the probabilities of performance within various ranges of return according to the investor's personal preferences.

---

[8]See Clarke (1987) and Brooks and Levy (1987) for a discussion of these results.

5. Option Contracts: Pricing Relationships

Because options are derivative securities, the price of an option depends on, among other things, the value of the underlying security. Some common option-pricing relationships and more formal valuation models are illustrated in this chapter.

Adjusted Intrinsic Value and Put/Call Parity

Chapter 4 discusses why the price of an option should be greater than or equal to its intrinsic value. In fact, the relationship is even tighter. For the call option, consider the strategy of buying a call option and investing $E/(1 + rT)$ dollars in a pure-discount, riskless bond that pays E dollars at maturity T and yields an annualized rate of return r over the period. The value matrix at maturity is shown below.

	$S < E$	$S > E$
Call	0	$S - E$
$E/(1 + rT)$	E	E
Total payoff	E	S

Because the total payoff at each point is greater than or equal to holding the security itself, the current value of the security must be less than or equal to the call option and the present value of the riskless bond; that is,

$$S_0 \leq C + E/(1 + rT),$$

or equivalently,

$$C \geq S_0 - E/(1 + rT),$$

where S_0 represents the current price of the security. Thus, the call option must be priced greater than or equal to the adjusted intrinsic value of the option. A similar relationship holds for the put option, but it is somewhat less restrictive.[9]

The next important pricing relationship is the arbitrage link, known as put/call parity. To understand this relationship, consider the investment strategy shown below.

	$S < E$	$S > E$
Security	S	S
Put	$E - S$	0
$-$Call	0	$-(S - E)$
Total payoff	E	E

The investor buys the security, buys a put, and sells a call with expiration T. The payoff from this strategy results in a fixed amount, E, whether the security price rises or falls. Because the payoff is certain, or fixed, no matter which way the security

---

[9]This relationship is illustrated in the exercises section of this tutorial.

price moves, the strategy is related to the annualized riskless rate, r, in the following way:

$$S_0 + P - C = \frac{E}{(1 + rT)},$$

where S_0 is the current security price. The left side of this equation represents an investment in the security and the options that pay off E dollars; the right side represents a pure-discount, riskless investment that also pays off E dollars at maturity. Because the two investments have the same payoff, they should sell for the same price.

This relationship between the security price, the price of the put, the price of the call, the exercise price of the option, and the riskless rate is known as put/call parity. It is this arbitrage relationship that keeps European options linked together with the underlying security price. If this relationship does not hold, then one could create greater-than-riskless returns with no risk by selling the expensive combination of assets and buying the cheap combination.

This important relationship is similar to the cash-and-carry arbitrage for futures contracts. It determines the fair price between the put and call options and the underlying security. It also serves as a guide to designing some option strategies.

The pricing relationships shown in Table 5.1 expand the list of characteristics referenced in Chapter 4.

The put/call parity relationship also gives some insight into the determinants of the time value of an option. Consider the case of the call option by starting with the put/call parity relationship and adding and subtracting the exercise price to form the following relationship:

$$C = S_0 - \frac{E}{1 + rT} + P$$

$$= (S_0 - E) + \left(E - \frac{E}{1 + rT}\right) + P.$$

$$\underset{\substack{\text{Intrinsic} \\ \text{Value}}}{} \qquad \underset{\substack{\text{Time} \\ \text{Value}}}{}$$

For a call option that is in the money, the first term represents the intrinsic value of the obligation to purchase the security for E dollars. The time value is composed of two additional terms. One represents the interest opportunity cost saved by waiting to exercise the call option, which is equal to the difference between the strike price and its present value. The higher the interest rate, the greater the benefit of waiting. The last term, P, is the price of a put option with the same exercise price. The put represents the value of being able to cancel the purchase if the security price drops to a level at which purchasing the security at the higher strike price is unfavorable for the investor. An adverse drop in price depends heavily on the volatility of the security. The higher the volatility, the greater the chance that the security price might drop below the strike price at expiration. Consequently, the time value of the option will depend importantly on the option's strike price, the current interest rate, and the security's volatility.

Notice that both terms composing the time value of a call option are positive. For a security with no cash distributions (dividends or interest, for example), the time value is always positive, which creates a call premium greater than intrinsic value. An investor has no incentive to exercise the call option early; early exercise gives a payoff

Table 5.1 Pricing Relationships

Relationship	Call Option	Put Option
Exercise price	$C(E_1) \geq C(E_2)$	$P(E_1) \leq P(E_2)$
Time to expiration	$C(T_1) \leq C(T_2)$	$P(T_1) \leq P(T_2)$
Intrinsic value	$C \geq \max(0, S_0 - E)$	$P \geq \max(0, E - S_0)$
Adjusted intrinsic value	$C \geq \max[0, S_0 - E/(1 + rT)]$	$P \geq \max\left[0, \dfrac{E}{(1 + rT)} - S_0\right]$
Put/call parity	$C = S_0 + P - E/(1 + rT)$	

Note: r = annualized riskless interest rate up to option expiration, S_0 = current price of the security, P = put option price, C = call option price, $T_1 < T_2$ = expiration relationship, and $E_1 < E_2$ = strike price relationship.

equal only to the intrinsic value and causes the investor to forfeit the outstanding time value.

As an illustration, suppose a call option has the following parameters:

$S_0 = \$100$ $E = \$95$ $r = 8$ percent
$T = 1/12$ year $C = \$6.43$ $P = \$0.80$

The intrinsic value of the call option $(S_0 - E)$ is $\$5.00$. The time premium of $\$1.43$ can be decomposed into $\$0.63$ for the interest opportunity cost $[E - E/(1 + rT)]$ and $\$0.80$ for the implied put option (P). Thus, the call option price is $\$6.43$.

The interpretation of the time premium for a put option is similar, except that the time value is not unambiguously positive. Rearranging the put/call parity relationship for the put option gives

$$P = -S_0 + E/(1 + rT) + C$$

$$= (E - S_0) - [E - E/(1 + rT)] + C.$$

| Intrinsic | Time |
| Value | Value |

For a put option that is in the money, the intrinsic value is given by the first term and represents the obligation to sell the security for E dollars. The second term represents the interest opportunity cost from not exercising the put option and investing the proceeds from the sale until expiration. The higher the interest rate, the greater the penalty for waiting to receive the proceeds of the option. The price of the call option with the same exercise price represents the value of being able to cancel the sale if the security price rises to a level at which selling the security at the lower strike price is unfavorable for the investor. The two time-value terms for the put option have opposite signs, however. If the put option goes so deep in the money that the price of the call option is small, the investor might have an incentive to exercise the put option early to capture the potential interest to be earned on the gain. For a European option, which cannot be exercised early, a put option deep in the money might actually have a negative time value.

Suppose a put option has the following parameters:

$S_0 = \$100$ $E = \$105$ $r = 8$ percent
$T = 1/12$ year $C = \$1.29$ $P = \$5.59$

The intrinsic value of the put option is $\$5.00$, and the time premium of $\$0.59$ is composed of $-\$0.70$ for the interest opportunity cost and $\$1.29$ for the implied call option.

Early Exercise of American Options

Put/call parity is also useful in examining the early exercise of an American option. Recall that exercising an American put early may be advantageous if the put is deep enough in the money. This can be shown through the put/call parity relationship:

$$P = \frac{E}{(1 + rT)} + C - S_0.$$

If $E - S_0 > P$, or (from the put/call parity relationship) $C < ErT/(1 + rT)$, then the payoff from early exercise is greater than the market value.

An investor would be willing to exercise the put early if the intrinsic value to be received upon exercise is greater than the fair value of the put. The put/call parity relationship indicates that the investor is better off exercising the put option if the put is so deep in the money that a call option with the same strike price is less than the present value of interest on the exercise price. In this case, the investor is better off exercising the put early and earning interest on the intrinsic value than retaining the put option itself.

Using the relationships above, Table 5.2 illustrates the approximate point at which an investor would be better off exercising the American put.

Table 5.2 Early Exercise for Put Option

Security Price	Put Price	$E - S_0$	Call Price
$100.00	$3.74	$ 0.00	$ 4.96
95.00	6.37	5.00	2.60
90.40	9.59	9.60	1.22 ←Early Exercise
90.00	9.90	10.00	1.13

Note: $E = \$100$, $r = 5\%$, $T = 1/4$ year, and $E_r T/(1 + rT) =$ $\$1.23$. Option prices are calculated using the Black-Scholes model with $\sigma = 22.0\%$.

As the security price drops from $100 to $90.40, the put price increases to the point at which the investor would do better to exercise early and earn interest on the option's intrinsic value than to continue to own the put. This point is reached when the price of a comparable call option is less than $1.23.

A similar situation exists for the possible early exercise of an American call option. Early exercise is desirable if the ex-dividend payoff from early exercise is greater than the ex-dividend value of the call option; that is, when

$$S_0 + D - E > C,$$

or rearranging, using the put/call parity relationship,

$$D > \frac{ErT}{(1 + rT)} + P.$$

The event triggering a possible early exercise of a call option is a cash distribution such as the payment of a dividend. If the dividend is large enough, exercising the option may be to the investor's advantage. The investor receives the security and the dividend instead of holding the call option while the security falls to its ex-dividend price. The investor is better off to exercise the call option early if the value of the call option using the ex-dividend price is less than the value the investor would receive by exercising early and capturing the dividend.

An interesting situation occurs if no dividend is to be paid before the maturity of the call option. In this case, the investor has no incentive to exercise the American option early, and it behaves as if it were a European option. The American call option in this case is said to be "worth more alive than dead." That is, exercising the call option early is not optimal if no cash distribution is to be made. Consequently, the American call option behaves as if it were European, even though it could be exercised early.

The case for early exercise of the American call option is illustrated in Table 5.3. The dividend is varied to the point at which exercising the call option early and capturing the dividend would be optimal. Notice that the dividend must rise to $2.25 before exercising the call option early is advantageous. Generally, exercising a call option is not going to be optimal unless the dividend is large and the call option is deep in the money.

Binomial Pricing Model

As noted earlier, the option price depends on the price of the underlying security. The price is also sensitive to the level of interest rates, volatility, and time to expiration. Once an investor knows exactly how an option is priced, he or she can tell how sensitive the price is to these other variables.

Figure 5.1 begins with a simple option-pricing framework. Suppose a security can only move up or down; the price is then designated as S_u or S_d, respectively. If the security's price goes up, the call option has a value C_u; if it goes down, the call option has a value C_d. The value of the call option if the security rises is the maximum of zero and $S_u - E$, and if the security falls, the value is the maximum of zero and $S_d - E$.

Suppose an investor constructs a hedge posi-

Table 5.3 Early Exercise for Call Option

D	Security Price	C	P	$P + ErT/(1 + rT)$
		Ex-dividend		
$ 0.00	$100.00	$11.85	$0.76	$1.87
1.00	99.00	10.99	0.90	2.01
2.00	98.00	10.15	1.06	2.17
2.25	97.75	9.94	1.10	2.21 ←Early Exercise
3.00	97.00	9.34	1.24	2.36
4.00	96.00	8.55	1.46	2.57
5.00	95.00	7.79	1.70	2.81

Note: $S_0 = \$100$, $E = \$95$, $r = 5\%$, and $T = 1/4$ year. Option prices are calculated using a Black-Scholes model with $\sigma = 22.0\%$.

Figure 5.1 Simple Binomial Pricing Model

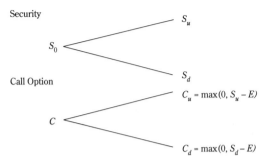

Security

S_0 — S_u

S_d

Call Option

C — $C_u = \max(0, S_u - E)$

$C_d = \max(0, S_d - E)$

tion so that the payoff B is the same no matter which way the security price moves. The initial position would be to hold the security, plus h units of the call option:

$$B_0 = S_0 + hC.$$

The hedge ratio, h, is chosen so that the ending payoff, or value B, is the same no matter which way the security price moves. Setting the two payoffs equal to each other allows the investor to find a value of h that will give the fixed payoff. So the ending payoff is

$$B = S_u + hC_u$$

$$= S_d + hC_d.$$

The hedge position creates a riskless payoff similar to the put/call parity relationship. Solving for h gives the value of the hedge ratio that will make the payoff the same whichever way the security price moves. The hedge ratio h is related to the difference in the security price as it moves either up or down and the corresponding difference in the payoff of the call option:

$$h = \frac{-(S_u - S_d)}{(C_u - C_d)}.$$

One other important thing should be noted about the hedge position. Because the ending payoff is fixed, or certain, it must be related to the annualized riskless rate r and maturity t. That is, the present value of the ending payoff B should be equal to the investment made to construct it:

$$B_0 = \frac{B}{(1 + rt)}.$$

Combining the relationship $B_0 = S_0 + hC$ and the two equations above to solve for the call price gives

$$C = \frac{qC_u + (1 - q)C_d}{(1 + rt)}.$$

This equation for the call option has been simplified somewhat by defining the variable q as follows:

$$q = \frac{S_0(1 + rt) - S_d}{S_u - S_d}.$$

The price of the call option is a function of the payoff on the call option if the security price goes up and the payoff if the security goes down. It is also a function of the level of interest rates and time to expiration t and is sensitive to the difference in the change in the price of the underlying security, up or down. The equation for the call option gives the price of the option to avoid arbitrage profits. If the option is worth less than this amount, the investor could make a return greater than the riskless rate with no risk. This possibility establishes a relationship between the price of the call option, the riskless rate of interest to maturity t, the current price of the security, and the movement of the security.

To illustrate how a call option is priced in this way, suppose the riskless rate of interest is 5 percent, the exercise price on the option is \$100, the maturity is one year, the current security price is \$100, and when the security moves it will either go up to \$110 (S_u) or down to \$95 (S_d). The payoff of the call option if the security price moves up gives an intrinsic value of \$10; if the security price goes down, the option is worth zero; that is,

$$C_u = \max(0, 110 - 100) = 10,$$

$$C_d = \max(0, 95 - 100) = 0.$$

First solve for q,

$$q = \frac{100(1.05) - 95}{110 - 95} = \frac{2}{3},$$

and then calculate the value of the call option

$$C = \frac{10\left(\frac{2}{3}\right) + 0\left(\frac{1}{3}\right)}{1.05} = 6.35.$$

45

The option must be priced at this level or an investor could make more than the riskless rate of return. The hedge ratio, h, between the security and the call option in this example is

$$h = \frac{(110 - 95)}{(10 - 0)} = \frac{3}{2},$$

which means that the initial portfolio the investor would construct would be to buy one security for $100 and sell 3/2 call options at $6.35 for each option. The cost of this portfolio is

$$B_0 = 100 - \frac{3}{2}(6.35) = \$90.48.$$

Constructing this portfolio composed of the security and the call options gives the same ending value as taking $90.48 and investing it in a riskless bond at a rate of 5 percent for one year. This creates an arbitrage relationship between the price of the call option, the price of the underlying security, and the riskless rate of interest. The option must be priced at $6.35 for that relationship to hold.

The pricing of a put option is similar to that of a call option, as illustrated in Figure 5.2. Again, the security price can move up or move down. The payoff of the put option is P_u or P_d. The investor constructs a hedge so that the payoff is fixed no matter which way the security price moves.

To construct the hedge, the investor buys the security and h units of the put option for an initial position of

$$B_0 = S_0 + hP.$$

The ending payoff from the portfolio is the same whichever way the security price moves:

Figure 5.2 Binomial Pricing of a Put Option

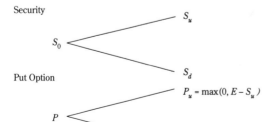

$$B_0 = S_u + hP_u$$
$$= S_d + hP_d.$$

Solving for h from the equation above gives the hedge ratio

$$h = \frac{-(S_u - S_d)}{(P_u - P_d)}.$$

Because the ending payoff is certain, it is related to the riskless rate in the same way

$$B_0 = \frac{B}{(1 + rt)}.$$

Combining equations allows one to solve for the put option price

$$P = \frac{qP_u + (1 - q)P_d}{(1 + rt)},$$

where

$$q = \frac{S_0(1 + rt) - S_d}{S_u - S_d}.$$

To illustrate the pricing of a put option, the same initial parameters are used as in the example of the call option. The payoff from the put option if the security price rises is

$$P_u = \max(0, 100 - 110) = 0.$$

The payoff from the put option if the security price falls is

$$P_d = \max(0, 100 - 95) = \$5.$$

The parameter q still has the value 2/3, so the value of the put option is

$$P = \frac{0\left(\frac{2}{3}\right) + 5\left(\frac{1}{3}\right)}{1.05} = 1.59.$$

The put option must have this value to maintain the arbitrage conditions. If the put option did not have this value, investors could earn rates of return greater than the riskless rate with no risk.

The hedge ratio for the put option is a little different from that for the call option. In the example for the put, the hedge ratio is

$$h = \frac{-(110 - 95)}{0 - 5} = 3.$$

To construct the hedge portfolio, an investor spends $100 for the security and buys three options, each worth $1.59; that is,

$$B_0 = 100 + 3(1.59) = \$104.77.$$

Thus, the investor could achieve a riskless return by investing $104.77 at the riskless rate for one year or by spending $104.77 to buy the security and three put options. Either combination would pay the same amount after the security price moves, and they could be considered equivalent investments.

Two-Period Binomial Pricing Model.

A slightly more complex model is one in which the security's price can move over two periods of time each of length t. This model is illustrated in Figure 5.3. In the first period, the security can go up to a price S_u or down to a price S_d. In the next period, if the security has gone up, it can go up again, to a price S_{uu} or down to a price S_{ud}. If the security has gone down in the first period, it can go up to a price S_{du} or down to a price S_{dd}. (For simplicity, we assume $S_{ud} = S_{du}$.)

Figure 5.3 Two-Period Model: Security Price Movement

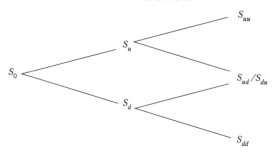

The movement in the call option price is illustrated in Figure 5.4. If the security price first goes up, the call option has a value of C_u; if it goes down, it has a value of C_d. In the next period, the security price can move up or down again, and the value of the option at that point will equal its intrinsic value at expiration.

Although this model is more complex than the one-period model, the arbitrage is similar. Suppose the security price has gone up, so the security price is at the point S_u. With one period left, the value of the call option can be determined. The investor knows the value, because he or she

Figure 5.4 Two-Period Model: Call Price Movement

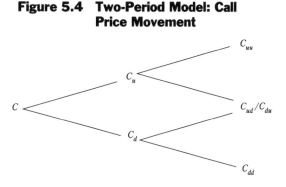

can construct a riskless hedge with one period to go. The one-period problem gives a well-determined price for the call option, which must hold to avoid the arbitrage possibilities.

Next, suppose the security price has gone down in the first period to S_d. The investor also knows what the value of the option must be at this point. With one period left, a riskless hedge can be constructed that determines what the value of the option must be. Knowing the option values at the intermediate points allows the investor to work backward to the initial period. The problem of evaluating the option with the security price at S_0 is now suitable to a one-period model with a well-defined value for the call option at the end of each branch.

This type of option-pricing model is solved by working backward. The process starts in the final time period and works back along each branch ultimately to solve the first-period problem. The formula for the value of a two-period call option is

$$C = \frac{qC_u + (1-q)\,C_d}{(1+rt)}$$

$$= \frac{q^2 C_{uu} + 2q(1-q)C_{ud} + (1-q)^2 C_{dd}}{(1+rt)^2}.$$

The first form of this equation is familiar. It is the value of a call option for which payoff in the next period is C_u and C_d. C_u and C_d, however, are also options that have payoffs in the subsequent period. Putting in the value for each of these options permits writing the equation in terms of the ultimate option values at the end of the second period (the second form of the equation). The value of a call option is a function of the current

47

interest rate in addition to the parameter q, which is defined the same as for the one-period model.[10]

As an example of the two-period call option, suppose the security can take on several values. If it goes up twice, it goes up from $100 to $110 and up again to $121. If it goes up to $110 and then down, or down and then up, the security price is $104.50. If the security price goes down twice, it goes down to $95 and then to $90.25. The exercise price of the option is $100, so the payoff of the call option at expiration if the security price goes up twice is $21. If the security price goes up and then down, the payoff is $4.50. If the security goes down twice, the payoff of the call option is zero, because at expiration the security price is less than the exercise price. To summarize, the final payoff at expiration is

$$C_{uu} = \max(0, S_{uu} - E) = \$21.00$$
$$C_{ud} = \max(0, S_{ud} - E) = \$4.50$$
$$C_{dd} = \max(0, S_{dd} - E) = \$0.00$$

By working backward, one can determine the option price at each intermediate point. When the security has gone up, the option (C_u) is worth $14.76. At that point, the hedge ratio to create a riskless hedge is -1. If the security goes down first, the value of the option (C_d) is $2.86. The hedge ratio used to construct a riskless hedge at that point is $-19/6$. Once these two values for the call option are known, the investor can work back and find the value of the call option at the beginning

---

[10] The parameter q is the same from one period to the next if the security always moves up by the same proportion and down by the same proportion each period. Otherwise, this equation is written as

$$C =$$

$$\frac{q[q_u C_{uu} + (1 - q_u) C_{ud}] + (1 - q) [q_d C_{du} + (1 - q_d) C_{dd}]}{(1 + rt)^2}.$$

The parameters q_u and q_d in the final period are not necessarily the same as q in the first period. They are given as

$$q_u = \frac{S_u(1 + rt) - S_{ud}}{S_{uu} - S_{ud}},$$

$$q_d = \frac{S_d(1 + rt) - S_{dd}}{S_{du} - S_{dd}}.$$

of the process. The call option is worth $10.28, with an initial hedge ratio of $-3/2$.

To illustrate a two-period put option, assume the security price moves in the same way as for the call option in the previous example. The payoff of the put option if the security price moves up twice in a row is zero. If the security price moves up and then down, the payoff is again zero. Only if the security price moves down twice in a row is the put option in the money, and the payoff is $9.75. That is,

$$P_{uu} = \max(0, E - S_{uu}) = \$0.00$$
$$P_{ud} = \max(0, E - S_{ud}) = \$0.00$$
$$P_{dd} = \max(0, E - S_{dd}) = \$9.75$$

At the intermediate period, the value of the put option (P_u) is zero if the security price has moved up or $3.10 if the security price has moved down (P_d). The value of the put option is zero if the security price moves up because at each point thereafter, the option is out of the money and has a zero payoff. Using these intermediate option values of zero and $3.10 after the first period, one can determine that the price of the option at the beginning (P) would be $0.98, with an initial hedge ratio of 4.84.

This simple binomial branching process allows an analyst to incorporate a wide range of complexities into the model. In particular, the analyst can adjust the option price for such things as dividend payments and the possibility of early exercise of the option. The framework is very flexible in adapting to particular constraints or conditions on the option.

For example, consider a put option with the possibility of early exercise at the intermediate points. The example here is exactly the same as that of the put option in the previous example except for the possibility that the option might be exercised early in the intermediate period. Checking for the desirability of early exercise at the intermediate points requires that the investor examine whether the unexercised value of the put is less than the intrinsic value of the put if exercised early. The put option prices with early exercise possible are

$$P_u = \max(0, E - S_u) = 0, \text{ and}$$
$$P_d = \max(3.10, E - S_d) = 5.00.$$

If the stock price falls to $95, the intrinsic value of the put is $100 - 95 = $5, which is greater than the unexercised put price of $3.10. Consequently, the investor would exercise the put early. This intrinsic value is then used to complete the pricing of the put in the first period, which gives P a value of $1.59 and a hedge ratio of 3 instead of a value of $0.98 and a hedge ratio of 4.84. The possibility of early exercise adds $0.61 to the price of the put option and lowers the hedge ratio.

Multiperiod Binomial Mode. Figure 5.5 illustrates a more complex model than the one or two periods illustrated previously. The mathematics will not be done here, but the logic behind the process can be sketched out. Suppose a security has many branches, but at each point, it can go up or down only by the same relative proportions each time. Using the mathematics for an increasingly complex branching network, the resulting call price takes on the form

$$C = S_0(\text{prob}_1) - E(1 + rt)^{-n}(\text{prob}_2),$$

where n is the number of periods in the branching process. The call price is a function of the current security price times a probability minus the present value of the exercise price of the option times a second probability. The two probabilities are given by the cumulative binomial distribution.

For those familiar with typical statistics and probability formulations, the binomial branching process for the security price is recognizable, and they will not be surprised that the probabilities come from the binomial probability distribution. The general form of the model results in a call price equal to the security price times a probability minus the present value of the exercise price times a probability. Obviously, the terms of the model could get quite complex as more and more steps are added, but the general form of the model can be represented by the equation above.

Black-Scholes Model

For a model in which the total time to expiration (T) for the option is constant but, because more branches are added, the total time interval is divided into smaller and smaller pieces, in the limit, the binomial process converges to the Black-Scholes model for a call option:

$$C = S_0 N(d_1) - E e^{-rT} N(d_2),$$

where

$$d_1 = \frac{\ln(S_0/E) + (r + \frac{1}{2}\sigma^2)\,T}{\sigma\sqrt{T}},$$

$$d_2 = d_1 - \sigma\sqrt{T}, \text{ and}$$

$N(d)$ = cumulative normal distribution.

The Black-Scholes model indicates that the call option is equal to the security price times a probability minus the present value of the exercise price times a probability. The probabilities are given by the cumulative normal distribution represented in Figure 5.6. The form of the Black-Scholes model is similar to that of the binomial model: the security price times a probability minus the present value of the strike price times a probability. The cumulative binomial probabilities are replaced by the cumulative normal distribution because in the limit, the binomial converges to the normal distribution.

One of the differences between the Black-Scholes formula and the equation underlying the two-period example is the present value factor. The previous present value factor represented

Figure 5.5 Multiperiod Model

Figure 5.6 Standard Normal Curve

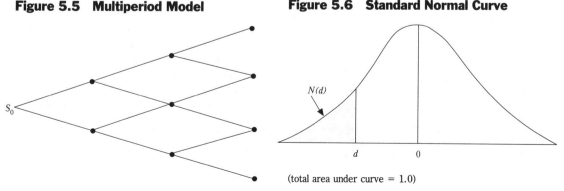

S_0

$N(d)$

d 0

(total area under curve = 1.0)

discrete compounding. In the limit, e^{-rT} is the continuous compounding equivalent of the discrete present value factor $(1 + rt)^{-n}$. Notice that the call price depends on the current security price and the exercise price; it also depends on the rate of interest (r), the time to expiration (T), and the risk of the underlying security (σ). In the simple binomial model, the uncertainty of the security price was represented by the size of the price movement of the security. In the more complex Black-Scholes model, that risk is represented by the volatility of return (σ), because the security can take on many values at expiration instead of only two.[11]

The price of the put option can be easily found from the Black-Scholes model by using the put/call parity relationship with continuous compounding

$$P = C - S_0 + Ee^{-rT}$$

$$= S_0[N(d_1) - 1] - Ee^{-rT}[N(d_2) - 1],$$

where d_1, d_2, and $N(d)$ are defined as in the Black-Scholes equation. Substituting in the price of the call option developed by Black-Scholes gives the price of the put option. The formula is similar to the call option formula: the security price times a probability minus the present value of the strike price times a probability. The associated probabilities are again drawn from the cumulative normal distribution. A table of values for the cumulative normal distribution is given in Appendix D, along with a numerical algorithm used to calculate the values.

Black-Scholes Model Option Pricing.

For an example of establishing option prices using the Black-Scholes model, assume the security price (S_0) is $100, the strike price (E) is also $100, the riskless rate (r) is 5 percent, and the volatility (σ) is 22 percent. For an option with a maturity (T) of one year, d_1 would equal 0.34; d_2, 0.12; $N(d_1)$, 0.6331; and $N(d_2)$, 0.5478. The price for the call option is

$$C = 100(0.6331) - 100(0.9512)(0.5478) = \$11.20,$$

and the price for the put option is

---

[11] The correspondence between the jump sizes up and down in a binomial model and the volatility in the Black-Scholes model is often specified as $u = \exp(\sigma\sqrt{T/n})$ and $d = 1/u$, where n is the number of periods in the binomial model, $S_u = uS_0$ and $S_d = dS_0$.

Table 5.4 Comparison of Binomial and Black-Scholes Models

Model	Days to Expiration	Call Option Exercise Price		
		45	50	55
Binomial	30	$5.38	$1.40	$0.07
($n = 5$)	120	6.74	3.21	1.12
Binomial	30	5.37	1.36	0.08
($n = 25$)	120	6.70	3.13	1.08
Black-Scholes	30	5.39	1.36	0.08
	120	6.75	3.15	1.09

Note: $S_0 = 50$, $r = 10\%$/year, and $\sigma = 20\%$/year.

$$P = 100(-0.3669) - 100(0.9512)$$
$$\times (-0.4522) = \$6.32.$$

For a call option with one-quarter of a year to expiration, d_1 equals 0.17; d_2, 0.06; $N(d_1)$, 0.5675; $N(d_2)$, 0.5239. The prices for the call and put options are

$$C = 100(0.5675) - 100(0.9876)(0.5239) = \$5.01,$$

$$P = 100(-0.4325) - 100(0.9876)$$
$$\times (-0.4761) = \$3.77.$$

Table 5.4 shows the relationship between a binomial model and the Black-Scholes model. A binomial model with only 5 branches and another binomial model with 25 branches can be used to compare the prices coming from the binomial model with those from the more complex Black-Scholes model (see Bookstaber 1985). The prices from the binomial models are very close to the Black-Scholes prices. Sometimes in option pricing, additional complexity does not make much difference. Most of the price differences are within a few cents of each other.

The use of an option-pricing model, such as the Black-Scholes, allows an investor to see how option prices respond to their parameters. The two curves in Figure 5.7 represent the prices of call and put options as the underlying security price varies. Both options have one month to expiration and an exercise price of $100. As the security price increases, the call option price also increases, which indicates that the option is more in the money than previously and is more valuable. The reverse is true for the put option: As the underlying security price increases, the put option becomes less valuable.

Figure 5.8 illustrates how the option price

Figure 5.7 Relationship of Option and Security Prices

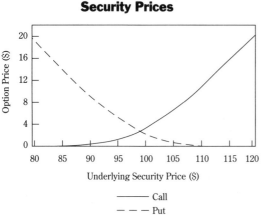

Underlying Security Price ($)

——— Call

— — — Put

Parameters: E = $100, T = 1 month, r = 5%, and σ = 22%.

changes as the time to expiration changes. These options are at the money, so all of the option premium is basically time value. For at-the-money options, the call option often has more time value than the put option, and the closer the option gets to expiration, the more the time value decays. Options are thus referred to as *wasting assets*; their time value falls to zero with the passage of time.

Figure 5.9 shows how the option price changes as the risk of the underlying asset changes. An option on a more risky asset is priced higher than an option on a less risky asset, as shown by the positive slope of the lines in the graph. The values

Figure 5.8 Relationship of Option Prices to Time to Expiration

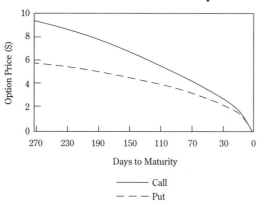

Days to Maturity

——— Call

— — — Put

Parameters: S_0 = $100, E = $100, r = 5%, and σ = 22%.

Figure 5.9 Relationship of Option Prices to Volatility

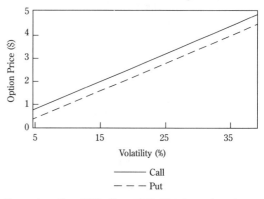

Volatility (%)

——— Call

— — — Put

Parameters: S_0 = $100, E_0 = $100, T = 1 month, and r = 5%.

of the options, both for the put and the call, increase as the volatility of the asset increases, because when the option is in the money, as volatility increases, the range of possible payoffs grows.

Figure 5.10 shows how an option price responds to an increase in interest rates. The price of the call option increases with an increase in interest rates, and the price of the put option decreases. This effect is consistent with the opportunity cost of early exercise implied in the time value of the put and call option prices discussed earlier.

Parameters for the Black-Scholes Model. The Black-Scholes model requires a

Figure 5.10 Relationship of Option Prices to Interest Rates

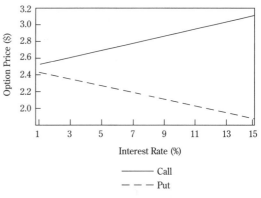

Interest Rate (%)

——— Call

— — — Put

Parameters: S_0 = $100, E = $100, T = 1 month, and σ = 22%.

51

knowledge of the current security price, the exercise price, the expiration date, the current interest rate, and the volatility of the underlying security. The first three parameters are well defined and readily observable. The interest rate generally used corresponds to a riskless rate with a horizon equal to the expiration date of the option. Strictly speaking, the interest rate should be a continuously compounded rate. Thus, to convert a simple annualized rate R to a continuously compounded rate r, the following relationship can be used:

$$\ln(1 + R) = r.$$

Although the continuously compounded rate will always be lower than the simple interest rate, any mispricing in the option caused by the use of the simple rate instead of the continuous rate will generally be small because the option price is not overly sensitive to the interest rate.

The volatility of returns for the underlying security is the last parameter in the model. It is represented by the standard deviation of the continuously compounded return on the security. In pricing options, analysts typically use some measure of historical volatility, such as daily, weekly, or monthly returns. If daily returns are used to estimate annual volatility, the daily variance is typically multiplied by 260 (trading days in a year) to obtain an annualized number. If weekly returns are used, the variance is multiplied by 52, or if monthly returns are used, the variance is multiplied by 12.

Alternatively, an analyst can use all the other inputs to the model to infer a volatility estimate from the actual market price of the option. This estimate of volatility is called the option's *implied volatility*. The volatility implied by the current option price can then be compared with historical volatility. Higher implied than historical volatility may indicate that the option is expensive relative to historical measures; lower implied volatility may indicate that the option is cheap. A fairly consistent pattern does seem to exist of reversion to the mean over time for volatility patterns: High implied volatilities tend to decline, and low volatilities tend to increase (see Bookstaber and Pomerantz 1989).

Table 5.5 illustrates the concept of implied volatility. The prices of both put and call options will vary as the volatility assumption changes. The

Table 5.5 Implied Volatility Using the Black-Scholes Model

Volatility Assumptions	Put Price	Call Price
.15%	$1.41	$2.04
.20	1.98	2.61
.25	2.55	3.18
.30[a]	3.11	3.74
.35	3.68	4.31

Note: $S_0 = \$100$, $E = \$100$, $r = 8\%$, and $T = 30$ days.
[a]Volatility implied by current option prices.

current market prices of the options correspond to a level of volatility of 30 percent a year. This percentage would be the level of volatility implied by current option prices in the example.

Assumptions. The Black-Scholes model depends upon several assumptions. It was originally developed under the assumption that returns for the security are log normally distributed and independent over time. In addition, it is assumed that the underlying security has constant risk, or variance, and that the interest rate is constant over time. The model also assumes no instantaneous price jumps in the security; that is, over a very short period of time, the security can move a little but not a large amount. The original model also assumed no dividends or cash payments from the security and no early exercise. The model was for pricing a European-style option. Researchers have tried to develop models to relax most of these assumptions. Many of today's models are variations of the original 1972 Black-Scholes model.

Of the binomial and Black-Scholes models, the more complex Black-Scholes was developed first. Only later did researchers think about the simple binomial model and realize that the simple model could be generalized into the Black-Scholes model (see Sharpe 1985, and Cox, Ross, and Rubinstein 1979).

The easiest assumption to relax is probably that of no cash distributions. If known dividends are to be paid on a stock before expiration of the option, the price of the option will adjust for the dividend payments. For known discrete dividends, the current stock price needs to be adjusted by the present value of the dividends before being used in the Black-Scholes model. For example, suppose the current stock price is S_0 with an expected dividend of D_t at time t. The adjusted stock price to use at each place in the Black-Scholes model to price the option is

$$S_0^* = S_0 - D_t e^{-rt}.$$

The incorporation of the dividend payment in a pricing model reduces the price of the call option and increases the price of a put option.

Another approach to adjusting the stock price is to assume that the dividend is paid continuously at a known yield (see Merton 1973). This assumption might approximate the dividends on a stock index; because of the many different stocks in an index, looking at each dividend separately is difficult. In this case, if d represents the aggregate annual dividend yield, the adjusted stock price used to price an option with expiration date T is

$$S_0^* = S_0 e^{-dT}.$$

Options on foreign exchange can also be put into this framework. In the case of foreign exchange options, the assumption is that the foreign currency pays continuous interest at rate r_f. The pricing of a foreign currency option could be found by using the Black-Scholes model with the following modification: If S_0 represents the current exchange rate, the modification involves substituting

$$S_0^* = S_0 e^{r_f T}$$

for each occurrence of S_0 in the standard Black-Scholes formula.

The dividend and foreign exchange adjustments presented here assume that the options cannot be exercised early, but variations of the Black-Scholes model for American options allow early exercise. Interested readers might consult Roll (1977), Geske (1979), and Whaley (1981). The techniques used to price American options are typically more complex than those for European options and require substantial numerical analysis for a solution.

Relaxing some of the other assumptions of the Black-Scholes model is more difficult than for those discussed here. Some attempts have been made to develop models in which the underlying security price is not log-normally distributed. For example, Bookstaber and McDonald (1985) have developed models with more general probability distributions, of which the log normal is a special

case. Relaxing the assumptions of constant variance and interest rates is yet more difficult. Specialized models for fixed-income options have been developed, however, by relaxing the assumption of constant interest rates (see Dattatreya and Fabozzi 1989, and Black, Derman, and Toy 1990).

Table 5.6 summarizes the modifications that can be made to the Black-Scholes model to price various types of European options.

Table 5.6 Modifications to the Black-Scholes Model

Discrete cash payout	$S_0^* = S_0 - D_t e^{-rt}$ D_t = payout at time t from the security
Continuous cash payout	$S_0^* = S_0 e^{-dt}$ d = rate of continuous payout or yield from the security
Currency option	$S_0^* = S_0 e^{-r_f T}$ r_f = foreign interest rate
Futures option	$S_0^* = F e^{-(r-d)T}$ F = futures price d = rate of continuous payout or yield from the security

Note: The standard Black-Scholes model can be used to price European options on securities with cash payouts, on currencies, or on futures contracts by substituting S_0^* for S_0 in the Black-Scholes formula.

Options on Futures

An option contract on a future differs from an option contract on the underlying security in that the buyer of the futures option, upon exercise, establishes a position in a futures contract instead of in the underlying security. In many respects, options on futures are not that different from cash options. An investor can think of the future as just another underlying security to which the option is tied.

Buyers of futures options must pay the full premium price. Sellers receive the premium, but, like sellers of regular options, are generally required to post margin. Upon exercise of a futures option, the investor is required to post margin and mark to market in order to maintain a position in the underlying futures contract. Many futures options expire on the same date as the underlying futures, although the Treasury bond and note futures options are an exception. They usually expire a month before the futures contract, so the investor can take full advantage of the delivery window for Treasury bond and note futures contracts.

The put/call parity relationship for European futures options is similar to that for cash options. A riskless payoff at time T can be constructed by buying a future, selling a futures call option, and buying a futures put option:

	$F_T < E$	$F_T > E$
Purchase future	$F_T - F$	$F_T - F$
Sell call	0	$-(F_T - E)$
Purchase put	$E - F_T$	0
Total payoff	$E - F$	$E - F$

Because the payoff from this strategy is riskless, the present value must equal the net amount of funds invested

$$P - C = \frac{E - F}{(1 + rT)},$$

or equivalently,

$$C = \frac{F - E}{(1 + rT)} + P.$$

The resulting put/call parity relationship is similar to that of cash options. Indeed, assuming the futures contract is priced like a forward contract, $F = S_0(1 + rT)$, if the futures price is substituted in terms of the cash, the result is

$$C = P + S_0 + \frac{F}{(1 + rT)},$$

which is simply the cash put/call parity relationship except that the put and call options are options on the futures contract.

This relationship introduces another point: If the futures options cannot be exercised early and the option and future expire at the same time, the European futures option is no different from a European cash option. This characteristic results from the fact that, at expiration, the futures price and cash price will be equal. That the futures price and security price are different before expiration does not matter if the futures option cannot be exercised early.

Fischer Black (1976) developed a variation of

the Black-Scholes model to apply to a European futures option:

$$C = [FN(d_1) - EN(d_2)]e^{-rT},$$

where

F = current futures price,

$$d_1 = \frac{\ln\left(\frac{F}{E}\right) + \frac{1}{2}\sigma^2 T}{\sigma\sqrt{T}},$$

$d_2 = d_1 - \sigma\sqrt{T}$, and

$N(d)$ = cumulative normal distribution.

Notice the similarity between the Black model and the Black-Scholes model. The Black model substitutes the present value of the futures price (using continuous compounding) for the cash price in the formula.

$$S_0^* = Fe^{-rT}.$$

With this substitution, the model can be used to price a European option on a futures contract.

The value for a European futures put option can be derived using the put/call parity relationship (using continuous compounding) along with the Black model for the value of the call option:

$$P = C + (E - F)e^{-rT}.$$

Using the value for the call option gives

$$P = (F[N(d_1) - 1] - E[N(d_2) - 1])e^{-rT},$$

where

$$d_1 = \frac{\ln\left(\frac{F}{E}\right) + \frac{1}{2}\sigma^2 T}{\sigma\sqrt{T}}, \text{ and}$$

$$d_2 = d_1 - \sigma\sqrt{T}.$$

Table 5.7 compares the price of European futures and cash options using the Black and Black-Scholes models. If the options and futures expire at the same time and there are no cash distributions from the underlying security, the options are priced the same.

One of the major differences between futures options and cash options occurs if the options can be exercised early. Recall that exercising an American call option on a security early was not desirable unless the cash distribution was large.

Table 5.7 Comparison of Cash and Futures Options

Option	Futures[a] Option Expiration		Cash[b] Option Expiration	
	1 Year	1/4 Year	1 Year	1/4 Year
Put	6.38	3.78	6.38	3.78
Call	11.14	4.98	11.14	4.98

Note: $E = \$100$, $r = 5\%$, and $\sigma = 22\%$.
[a]Current futures prices are assumed to be: $F_1 = \$105.00$, $F_{.25} = \$101.25$.
[b]The current security price is assumed to be: $S_0 = \$100$.

Exercising the American call and put futures options early may be desirable, however.

Exercising a futures call option early is desirable if the payoff from early exercise is greater than the value of the option; that is,

$$F - E > C.$$

Substituting for the value of the call option using put/call parity gives

$$P < rT(F - E)e^{-rt}.$$

This relationship can hold if the call option is far enough in the money to result in a small put price. If the call option is American, it would pay to exercise it at this point.

Exercising a futures put option early is desirable if the payoff from early exercise is greater than the value of the option; that is,

$$E - F > P.$$

Substituting for the value of the put option using put/call parity gives

$$C < rT(E - F)e^{-rt}.$$

This relationship can hold if the put option is far enough in the money to result in a small call price. If the put option is American, it would pay to exercise it at this point.

If the put and call options are deep enough in the money, time premiums are small and the option value is dominated by its intrinsic value. The interest available to be earned on the intrinsic value makes exercising the futures options early worthwhile; the investor thereby loses the time value of the option but gains the opportunity cost of the intrinsic value. Examples of the early exercise points for a put and call are shown in Table 5.8 and Table 5.9, respectively.

Pricing models for American futures options have been developed by Whaley (1986) and others. The prices of American futures options resulting from these models are usually somewhat higher than those given by the Black model for European options, because the possibility of early exercise is valuable to the investor.

Table 5.8 Early Exercise for Put Option on a Future: Example

Futures Price	$E - F$	Put Price	Call Price	$rT(E - F)e^{-rt}$
$100	$ 0	$ 4.33	$4.33	$0.00
95	5	7.14	2.21	0.06
90	10	10.81	0.93	0.12
85	15	15.13	0.31	0.19
83	17	16.98	0.18	0.21←Early Exercise
80	20	19.83	0.08	0.25

Note: $E = \$100$, $r = 5\%$, $T = 1/4$ year, and $\sigma = 22\%$.

Table 5.9 Early Exercise for Call Option on a Future

Futures Price	$F - E$	Call Price	Put Price	$rT(F - E)e^{-rt}$
$100	$ 0	$ 4.33	$4.33	$0.00
105	5	7.34	2.40	0.06
110	10	11.09	1.22	0.12
115	15	15.38	0.56	0.19
120	20	20.00	0.24	0.25 ←Early Exercise
121	21	20.95	0.20	0.26
125	25	24.79	0.10	0.31

Note: $E = \$100$, $r = 5\%$, $T = 1/4$ year, and $\sigma = 22\%$.

6. Short-Term Behavior of Option Prices: Hedging Relationships

This chapter describes some of the techniques used to monitor option positions and manage exposure in a portfolio. The first section describes how an option price moves as its parameters change. The second section addresses the use of these measures of price movement to help control the risk in a portfolio. The final section explores some alternative ways to create optionlike effects in a portfolio.

Sensitivity Measures

To describe how a call option price changes as its parameters change, the Greek notation shown in Table 6.1 is needed. The first is *delta* (Δ). It describes the change in the price of the option with respect to a change in the price of the underlying security. This measure is one of the most common and frequently used in managing an option position.

The second measure is *gamma* (γ). The delta itself is not a constant, and it will change as the security price changes. Gamma measures how quickly the delta changes as the security price changes.

The third measure is *theta* (θ). It is a measure of how the option price changes with the passage of time. The usual definition puts a negative sign in front because the option price increases with a

Table 6.1 Call Option Sensitivity Measures

Measure	Notation
Security Price	$\Delta_c = \dfrac{\partial C}{\partial S}$
Delta Sensitivity	$\gamma_c = \dfrac{\partial^2 C}{\partial S^2}$
Time to Expiration	$\theta_c = \dfrac{-\partial C}{\partial T}$
Interest Rates	$\rho_c = \dfrac{\partial C}{\partial r}$
Volatility	$\nu_c = \dfrac{\partial C}{\partial \sigma}$

longer time to expiration. The minus sign is a reminder that the option price will decay, or decrease, as the option nears expiration.

The next symbol is *rho* (ρ). It measures the sensitivity of the option price with respect to a change in interest rates.

The last measure is usually referred to as *vega* (ν) (or sometimes *kappa* [κ]). It measures the sensitivity of the option price with respect to the change in risk, or volatility, of the underlying security.

Delta. The delta on a call option is related to the delta on a put option, as can be seen using the put/call parity relationship with continuous compounding

$$C = S_0 + P - Ee^{-rt}.$$

Measuring the change of each side of the equation as the security price changes indicates how the option price will vary; that is,

$$\Delta_c = \Delta_s + \Delta_p$$

$$= 1 + \Delta_p,$$

or equivalently,

$$\Delta_p = \Delta_c - 1.$$

The delta of the risk-free asset in the equation is zero. It does not change as the security price changes. Consequently, the delta of the call option is equal to the delta of the security plus the delta of the put option. The delta of the security will be equal to 1 because its price changes one for one by definition. Therefore, the delta of the put option can be written as equal to the delta of the call option minus 1. The delta of the call option is positive and usually less than 1. Consequently, the delta of the put option will be negative.

Table 6.2 shows the formulas for each of the sensitivity measures of an option from the Black-Scholes model. Notice that the gammas and vegas are the same for both put and call options. Delta, theta, and rho are each different for the put and call options.

The beta of a stock option and the duration of a bond option are related to the delta of their respective options. The delta measures the price sensitivity of the option to the underlying security price, and beta and duration are related to relative percentage changes in price. The beta of an equity call option is related to the beta of the underlying security and the delta of the option in the following fashion:

$$\beta_c = \frac{\Delta_c \beta_s S_0}{C},$$

where

Δ_c = Call option delta,
β_s = Security beta,
S_0 = Security price, and
C = Call option price.

The modified duration of a bond call option is related to the modified duration of the underlying security and the delta of the call option:

$$D_c^* = \frac{\Delta_c BD_B^*}{C},$$

where D_B^* is the modified duration of the security, and B is the security price.

The beta and duration for a put option have a similar form and can be found by substituting the delta and price of the put option for that of the call option.

Figure 6.1 is a graph of the deltas of a call option and a put option with respect to the underlying security price, using the Black-Scholes model. When the call option is out of the money, the delta is close to 0. As the call option approaches the point of being in the money, the delta changes quickly and then approaches 1. A positive delta indicates that as the underlying security price

Table 6.2 Option Sensitivity Measures Using the Black-Scholes Model

Option Sensitivity to:	Call Option[a]	Put Option
Security price	$\Delta_c = N(d_1)$	$\Delta_p = \Delta_c - 1$
Delta	$\gamma_c = \dfrac{n(d_1)}{S\sigma\sqrt{T}}$	$\gamma_p = \gamma_c$
Time to expiration	$\theta_c = \dfrac{-S\sigma n(d_1)}{2\sqrt{T}} - rEe^{-rT}N(d_2)$	$\theta_p = \theta_c + rEe^{-rT}$
Interest rate	$\rho_c = ETe^{-rT}N(d_2)$	$\rho_p = \rho_c - ETe^{-rT}$
Volatility	$v_c = S\sqrt{T}\,n(d_1)$	$v_p = v_c$

[a]$n(d) = \dfrac{e^{-d^2/2}}{\sqrt{2\pi}}.$

Figure 6.1 Delta and Underlying Security Price Relationship

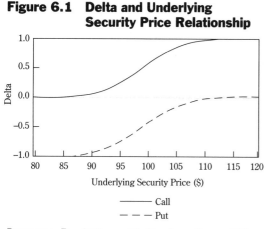

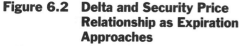

———— Call

— — — Put

Parameters: E = $100, r = 5%, T = 1 month, σ = 22%.

goes up, the price of the call option also goes up. Note the constant gap between the delta of the call and the delta of the put, which occurs because the delta of the put option is equal to the delta of the call option minus 1.

Deltas are also sensitive to the time to expiration of the option. Figure 6.2 shows how the shape of the delta profile changes slightly as the option expiration is changed. The delta curve tends to flatten out with longer option maturities.

Gamma. Knowledge about an option's delta is important because it allows the investor to measure how sensitive the option price is to changes in the security price.

Figure 6.2 Delta and Security Price Relationship as Expiration Approaches

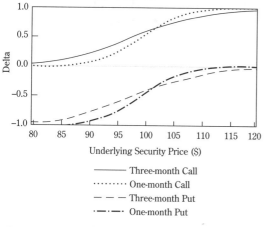

———— Three-month Call

········· One-month Call

— — — Three-month Put

·—·—· One-month Put

Parameters: E = $100, r = 5%, σ = 22%.

Figure 6.3 Gamma and Security Price Relationship

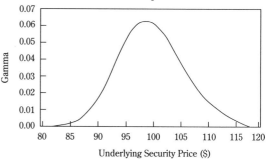

Parameters: E = $100, r = 5%, T = 1 month, σ = 22%.

Figure 6.3 shows a plot of the gamma of the same option, measuring how quickly delta is changing. At the extremes, when the option is way out of the money or way in the money, the delta does not change much and the gamma is small. When the option gets close to being at the money, the gamma is at its largest point. This position implies that the delta changes quickly as the security price changes. At its peak, the gamma indicates that, for a 1-point move in the underlying security, the delta changes by slightly more than 0.06. Consequently, if the delta happened to be 0.50, the delta would increase to 0.56 for a 1-point increase in the security price.

The gamma is also sensitive to the expiration period of the option. Figure 6.4 shows how the gamma curve flattens with longer times to the

Figure 6.4 Gamma and Security Price Relationship as Expiration Approaches

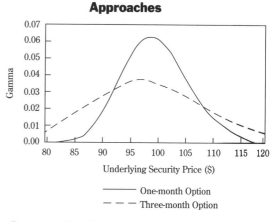

———— One-month Option

— — — Three-month Option

Parameters: E = $100, r = 5%, σ = 22%.

Figure 6.5 Theta and Security Price Relationship

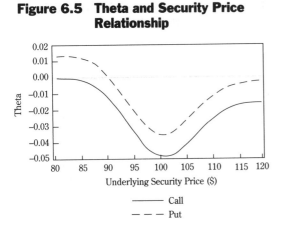

Parameters: E = $100, r = 5%, T = 1 month, σ = 22%.

Figure 6.6 Theta and Security Price Relationship as Expiration Approaches

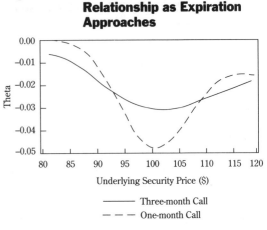

Parameters: E = $100, r = 5%, σ = 22%.

option's expiration. Gamma is the same for both the put and the call options.

Theta. Figure 6.5 shows the sensitivity of the option price to time decay, or the time to expiration. The call option is somewhat more sensitive than the put option at the same security price. For example, at its extreme point, the call option would lose about $0.05 a day in value, while the put option would lose less than $0.04 a day. The most sensitive area in time decay occurs when the option is at or close to the money; time decay is less pronounced when the option is way out of the money or way in the money.[12]

Time decay is also sensitive to the expiration date of the option, as shown in Figure 6.6. Time decay is most severe for short-term options close to the money.

Rho. Figure 6.7 shows rho—the sensitivity of the option price to a change in interest rates. When the security is way out of the money, the call option shows little sensitivity to a change in interest rates. Sensitivity increases when the option is in the money. The rho indicates that, at a price of $100, a 1 percent increase in the interest rate would increase the call option price by a little less than $0.04. Interest rate sensitivity for the

put option is negative, implying that put prices decrease with an increase in interest rates. The put option is more sensitive when it is in the money than when it is out of the money.

Interest rate sensitivity is also a function of the time to expiration of the option, as shown in Figure 6.8. The longer the expiration of the option, the more sensitive it is to a change in interest rates.

Vega. Figures 6.9 and 6.10 illustrate the sensitivity of the option price to the underlying security's volatility. The most sensitive area for the option is close to the money. When the option is out of the money or way in the money, it has little sensitivity to changes in underlying risk. This

Figure 6.7 Rho and Security Price Relationship

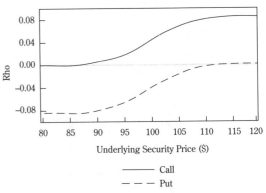

Parameters: E = $100, T = 1 month, r = 5%, σ = 22%.

---

[12]Figure 6.5 shows that the time decay goes positive for the put option when it is deep in the money. This relationship would be true for a European put option, but an American put option would be exercised early to capture the opportunity cost of the intrinsic value and avoid the negative time value in the put option.

Figure 6.8   Rho and Security Price Relationship as Expiration Approaches

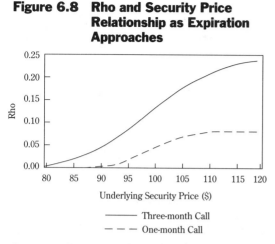

Underlying Security Price ($)

——— Three-month Call
– – – One-month Call

Parameters: E = $100, *r* = 5%, σ = 22%.

Figure 6.10   Vega and Security Price Relationship as Expiration Approaches

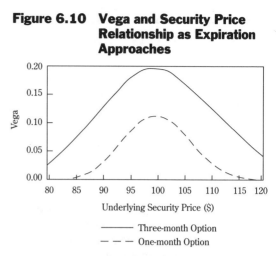

Underlying Security Price ($)

——— Three-month Option
– – – One-month Option

Parameters: E = $100, *r* = 5%, σ = 22%.

relationship occurs, because when the option is way out of the money, it has to move a long way before it ever pays off. Similarly, when the option is way in the money, it has to move a long way before it is worthless. When the option price is close to the strike price, whether the option will be worth something at expiration is uncertain, so its sensitivity to changes in volatility increases. The measure of volatility is the same for the put option as for the call option.

Vega is also sensitive to the maturity of the option. Long-term options are much more sensitive to changes in volatility than are shorter term options. For example, when at the money, a three-month option would increase in price by nearly $0.20 for a 1 percent increase in volatility, while a one-month option would increase by just over $0.10.

Figure 6.9   Vega and Security Price Relationship

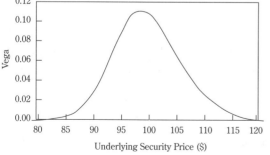

Underlying Security Price ($)

Parameters: E = $100, *r* = 5%, *T* = 1 month, σ = 22%.

Sample Sensitivity Measures. Table 6.3 shows some sample sensitivity measures for various strategies using the Black-Scholes model. The delta of the call option is 0.54—the delta when the option is at the money. The meaning of a delta of 0.54 is that, if the security price increases by $1, the call option will increase by $0.54. The movement of the price of the call option will be about half as much as the movement of the underlying security when the option is at the money.

The gamma of the call option is 0.06; that is, when the security price increases by $1, delta will increase by 0.06 and the option will be more sensitive to changes in the security price.

The theta is −0.05; when the time to maturity decreases by one day, the option price will decrease by $0.05. Theta is measuring the time decay of the option price.

Rho is 0.04: For a 1 percent increase in interest rates, the call price will increase by $0.04.

The vega of the call option is 0.11, indicating that, for a 1 percent increase in volatility of the security, the option price will increase by $0.11.

The values for a put option are also listed. It has a negative delta, a positive gamma, and a negative rho.

Table 6.3 also shows the parameters for several other strategies. The covered call has a delta of 0.46, indicating that, for a $1 increase in security value, the portfolio increases by $0.46. The gamma is negative, meaning that delta decreases as the security price rises, because the

Table 6.3 Sample Sensitivity Measures

Strategy	Delta	Gamma	Theta	Rho	Vega
Call option	0.54	0.06	−0.05	0.04	0.11
Put option	−0.46	0.06	−0.04	−0.04	0.11
Covered call	0.46	−0.06	0.05	−0.04	0.11
Protected put	0.54	0.06	−0.04	−0.04	0.11
Straddle	0.08	0.13	−0.08	0.00	0.23
Bull call spread	0.29	0.01	−0.01	0.02	0.02
Bear call spread	−0.28	0.02	−0.01	−0.03	0.04

Note: $S = E = \$100$, $r = 5\%$, $T = 30$ days, $\sigma = 22\%$.

covered-call strategy has sold off the upside potential of the security. Thus, the higher the security price, the more the delta decreases and the less responsive it is to a change in the security price. The theta of the covered-call position is positive; it gains rather than loses value as time passes. The vega is also negative, indicating that an increase in volatility in the market will hurt the value of the covered-call position.

The delta of the bull call spread, only 0.29, is smaller than those of the covered call or protected put, and because the gamma is small at this point, the delta does not change much. The theta is low, so the position does not have much time decay. The rho and the vega are also small; the value has little sensitivity to changes in interest rates or changes in volatility in the market.

Risk Control Using Sensitivity Measures

The sensitivity measures help describe the risk exposure of the investment position. Intuitively, the investor often knows the amount of risk to

which he or she is exposed, but these measures help quantify how much risk is in an investment position. Thus, they help the investment manager monitor and manage the risk of the portfolio.

Table 6.4 illustrates the relative importance of the various parameters, which are the same as in the previous examples. The change in the price of a call option is calculated using each parameter's volatility over a one-month period. For example, the security price has a variability over the course of a year of $22 and a one-month variability of $6.35. If the option has a delta of 0.58, the option price would have a one-month variability of $6.35(0.58) = 3.68$. Most of the expected price movement in the option is the result of a change in security price and the passage of time. Changes in volatility and interest rates generally have a smaller effect.

Because the option position is the most sensitive to changes in the underlying security price, the delta is often used in managing the underlying risk in an investment position. The delta of the security itself is

Table 6.4 Relative Importance of Option Sensitivities

Option Parameter	Annual Variability of Parameter	One-month Variability of Parameter	Call Option Price Sensitivity	Price Sensitivity times One-Month Variability
Security price	$22	$6.35	$\Delta_c = 0.58$	$3.68
Volatility	5%	1.4%	$v_c = 0.22$	0.31
Interest rates	3%	0.9%	$\rho_c = 0.17$	0.15
Time to expiration	365 days	30 days	$\theta_c = -0.03$	−0.90

Note: $S = E = \$100$, $r = 5\%$, $T = 1/4$ year, $\sigma = 22\%$. Annual variability represents the standard deviation of each parameter. One-month variability is equal to annual variability divided by $\sqrt{12}$ with the exception of the time to expiration.

$$\Delta_s = \frac{\partial S}{\partial S} = 1,$$

the delta of the call option is

$$\Delta_c = \frac{\partial C}{\partial S}, \text{ and}$$

the delta of the put option is related to the delta of the call option as follows:

$$\Delta_p = \frac{\partial P}{\partial S} = \frac{\partial C}{\partial S} - \frac{\partial S}{\partial S} = \Delta_c - 1.$$

Suppose an investor has a portfolio (V) consisting of one unit of Asset 1 and h units of Asset 2; that is, $V = I_1 + hI_2$. The change in the value of the portfolio as the security price changes is

$$\frac{\partial V}{\partial S} = \frac{\partial I_1}{\partial S} + h\frac{\partial I_2}{\partial S},$$

or in terms of delta,

$$\Delta_V = \Delta_1 + h\Delta_2.$$

The hedge ratio, h, which gives the amount of Asset 2 to hold relative to Asset 1 so as to give a desired net delta for the investment position as a whole, is similar to the hedge ratio calculated for futures contracts:

$$h = \frac{\Delta_V - \Delta_1}{\Delta_2}.$$

A special case of hedging occurs when the desired net delta (Δ_V) of the portfolio is 0—a hedge often called a *delta-neutral hedge*. In this case, the hedge ratio equals minus the delta of Asset 1 divided by the delta of Asset 2. To create a delta-neutral hedge, an investor would hold h units of Asset 2 for every unit of Asset 1;

$$h = \frac{\Delta_V - \Delta_1}{\Delta_2}$$

$$= \frac{-\Delta_1}{\Delta_2}.$$

To illustrate this concept, suppose Asset 1 is a call option and Asset 2 is the underlying security. The delta of Asset 1 is the delta of the call option ($\Delta_1 = \Delta_c$), and the delta of Asset 2 is equal to 1 ($\Delta_2 = 1$). To construct a delta-neutral hedge, the investor would hold h units of the security, where

$$h = \frac{-\Delta_1}{\Delta_2} = \frac{-\Delta_c}{1} = -\Delta_c.$$

If the delta of the call option is equal to 0.5, then the hedge ratio is −0.5, which means that, for every call option held, the investor should sell half a unit of the underlying security. When the underlying security increases by $1, the call option increases by $0.50 and the short security position loses $0.50 of value. The net effect is no change in the value of the portfolio—that is, a delta-neutral hedge. Of course, the delta of the call option is not constant, so once the security price begins to change, the ratio might have to be adjusted to keep a delta-neutral position.

For another example, suppose Asset 1 is a put option and Asset 2 is the associated call option. The delta of the put option is equal to the delta of the call option minus 1, or $\Delta_1 = \Delta_p = \Delta_c - 1$. The delta-neutral hedge ratio is

$$h = \frac{-\Delta_1}{\Delta_2} = \frac{1 - \Delta_c}{\Delta_c}.$$

If the delta of the call option is 0.5, the hedge ratio to construct a delta-neutral position is $(1 - 0.5)/0.5$, or 1. To create a delta-neutral hedge, the investor buys one call option for each put option held.

As the security price goes up, the call increases in value and the put loses value. The investor would hold the put and call in the right proportions to keep the total value from changing. This strategy creates a delta-neutral hedge between two separate options.

Consider one last example. Instead of a delta-neutral position, the investor desires a positive delta position of 2.0. Suppose the first asset is the security and the second asset is the call option. The hedge ratio to create a positive delta position is

$$h = \frac{\Delta_V - \Delta_1}{\Delta_2} = \frac{2 - 1}{\Delta_c}.$$

If the delta of the call option is equal to 0.5, then the hedge ratio is equal to $(2 - 1)/0.5$, or 2. To create a delta of 2 in the portfolio, the investor purchases two call options for each unit of the security held. For a $1 increase in the security price, the portfolio value increases by $2.

Option prices change in response to changes in

parameters other than the underlying security price. A change in interest rates, volatility, and the passage of time also cause the option prices to move slightly. Over a short period of time, a change in volatility is probably the next most important parameter after security price. Recall that both market direction and the cost of the option (represented by implied volatility) are critical in helping formulate successful option strategies. The reason is that a change in volatility can reinforce or negate much of the change in option price resulting from a change in the security price. So even though an investor may be correct in assessing market direction, the investment position may still be unprofitable if volatility changes in an adverse way.

The general framework for showing the total change in option price as the option's parameters change is

$$\Delta C = (\Delta_c + \tfrac{1}{2}\gamma_c \Delta S)\Delta S + \rho_c \Delta r + \nu_c \Delta \sigma - \theta_c \Delta T,$$

where

ΔC = change in call option price,
ΔS = change in security price,
Δr = change in interest rates,
$\Delta \sigma$ = change in volatility,
ΔT = change in time to expiration,
Δ_c = delta,
γ_c = gamma,
ρ_c = rho,
ν_c = vega, and
θ_c = theta.

The change in the price of a call option can be split into separate pieces resulting from a change in the underlying security price, the interest rate, time to expiration, and volatility. For price changes over a short period of time, the effect of the passage of time (ΔT) can be assumed to be negligible. Because the option's delta can change rapidly when the option is close to the money, the equation uses gamma to capture the second-order effect of a change in delta. The total change in the option's price is the sum of its response to changes in each parameter. Depending on which parameters change and by how much, some elements could offset others in their effects. For example, if

$\Delta S = \$1.00,$
$\Delta \sigma = -6.0$ percent,
$\Delta r = 0.5$ percent,
$\Delta T = -1$ day,
$\Delta_c = 0.54,$
$\gamma_c = 0.07,$
$\rho_c = 0.04,$
$\nu_c = 0.11,$ and
$\theta_c = -0.05,$

then $\Delta C = 0.58 - 0.02 - 0.66 - 0.05 = -\$0.15$. The increase in the option's price from the security price is more than offset by a decline in the volatility and time decay.

To hedge the option's total price movement would require that all of the parameters, not just the portfolio's delta, be controlled. Many times, however, the other parameters are ignored because their effects are generally smaller than a change in security price as captured by delta, but a more precise hedge can be constructed by also controlling for the effects of the other parameters.

The sensitivity of the total portfolio position is the sum of the sensitivities of each of the pieces in the portfolio. For example, the delta of the portfolio is equal to the sum of the deltas of each part of the portfolio. The ability to construct a portfolio that hedges against changes in volatility and interest rates thus requires the addition of other investment positions to the portfolio. For example, in Table 6.5, the ability to control a portfolio's

Table 6.5 Hedging Total Price Movement

Option Parameter to be Hedged	Sensitivity Measure Controlled	Total Hedge Position Sensitivity[a]
Security price		
First order	Delta	$\Delta_V = \Delta_1 + h_2\Delta_2 + h_3\Delta_3 + h_4\Delta_4 + h_5\Delta_5$
Second order	Gamma	$\gamma_V = \gamma_1 + h_2\gamma_2 + h_3\gamma_3 + h_4\Delta_4 + h_5\Delta_5$
Volatility	Vega	$\nu_V = \nu_1 + h_2\nu_2 + h_3\nu_3 + h_4\nu_4 + h_5\Delta_5$
Interest rates	Rho	$\rho_V = \rho_1 + h_2\rho_2 + h_3\rho_3 + h_4\rho_4 + h_5\rho_5$

[a]h_i = the hedge ratio for security i.

gamma, rho, and vega requires the use of an additional option position of somewhat different sensitivity for each parameter. If only the delta is to be controlled, two investment positions are needed. If both the delta and gamma are to be controlled, three positions are required, two of which must be options with dissimilar sensitivities. The ability to control each additional sensitivity measure requires an additional option position.

Table 6.6 illustrates the hedge ratios needed to create a delta/gamma-neutral hedge using two options and the underlying security. The problem requires the solution of a set of simultaneous equations, one equation for each of the parameters to be controlled, as illustrated in Table 6.5. Notice that the delta and gamma totals of the portfolio are constructed to be zero, while the vega is negative and the rho is positive because they are left unhedged. Table 6.6 also illustrates the hedge ratios required for a delta/gamma/vega-neutral hedge. Three simultaneous equations must be solved to find the hedge ratios for this problem. Notice again that the total portfolio sensitivity is constructed to be zero for each of the controlled parameters—delta, gamma, and vega—and the rho of the portfolio is left unhedged.

Alternative Ways to Create Option Effects

Several techniques can be used to generate optionlike effects in investment positions. The first technique uses the put/call parity relationship to create synthetic securities. In the familiar form of the put/call parity relationship, the call option can be thought of as being equal to the underlying security plus the put option less a cash-equivalent security or riskless bond; that is, $C = S_0 + P - [E/(1 + rT)]$. The combination of securities on the right side should perform the same way as the call option. Consequently, a call option can be created by buying the security, buying a put option, and borrowing money to do so. This combination would behave like the call option in its payoff or risk/return structure.

An investor also might create a synthetic put option through the put/call parity relationship. Rearranging the put/call parity equation so that

Table 6.6   Hedging Total Price Movement

	Sensitivity Measure			
	Δ	γ	ν	ρ
Security	1.0	0.0	0.0	0.0
Option 1	0.54	0.06	0.11	0.04
Option 2	0.75	0.03	0.16	0.08
Option 3	−0.32	0.04	0.08	−0.03
Instrument	h	$h \times \Delta$	$h \times \gamma$	$h \times \nu$	$h \times \rho$
Delta/Gamma-Neutral Hedge					
Security	1.0	1.0	0.0	0.0	0.0
Option 1	1.04	0.56	0.06	0.11	0.04
Option 2	−2.08	−1.56	−0.06	−0.33	0.17
Total		0.0	0.0	−0.22	0.21
Delta/Gamma/Vega-Neutral Hedge					
Security	1.0	1.0	0.0	0.0	0.0
Option 1	−0.90	−0.49	−0.06	−0.10	−0.04
Option 2	−0.08	−0.06	0.0	−0.01	−0.01
Option 3	1.40	−0.45	0.06	0.11	−0.04
Total		0.0	0.0	0.0	−.09

$P = [E/(1 + rT)] + C - S_0$ indicates that the put option is equal to the Treasury bill plus a call option and a short position in the underlying security. The combination of securities on the right-hand side would produce the same risk/return payoff as buying the put option directly.

The payoff of the underlying security can be replicated by buying a riskless bond, buying a call option, and selling a put option; that is, $S_0 = [E/(1 + rT)] + C - P$. This combination would behave like the underlying security. In a similar way, a riskless bond could be constructed by buying the underlying security, buying a put option, and selling a call option: $E/(1 + rT) = S_0 + P - C$. This latter combination of securities is how the put/call parity relationship was created earlier. Unless this relationship holds, riskless returns in excess of market rates could be generated.

To create a synthetic covered-call position, the put/call parity relationship may be rearranged as $S_0 - C = [E/(1 + rT)] - P$. On the left side, the covered-call position is traditionally created by buying the security and selling the call option. An equivalent way to do this is to buy a riskless bond and sell a put option.

For a synthetic protective put, rearrange the put/call parity relationship so that $S_0 + P = [E/(1 + rT)] + C$. The traditional protective put is constructed by buying the security and buying a put option. Another way to create a protective put is to buy a riskless bond and a call option. This technique is sometimes referred to as a 90/10 strategy, because approximately 90 percent of the investor's money is used to buy a riskless bond and 10 percent is used to buy call options. If the options expire worthless, the investor still has the principal safe in the bond, which creates a floor similar to buying a put option on the security.

These synthetic relationships are sometimes useful because constructing a particular payoff pattern may be easier using one particular combination of securities than another. Knowing how to use the put/call parity relationship gives an investor a choice of ways to create asset positions.

A second way to create optionlike effects is accomplished by trading frequently between a risky security and cash. This method is sometimes called *dynamic option replication*. Suppose an investor wants to replicate a put or call option using a portfolio of other assets. The replicating portfolio consists of the underlying security and a riskless bond or cash-equivalent security such as a Treasury bill. The movement of the replicating portfolio depends on how much of the money is put in the security and how much is in the cash equivalent. The proportion of money put with the underlying security is represented by alpha. Thus, the replicating portfolio and its delta are

$$R = \alpha S + (1 - \alpha) \text{ cash}$$
$$\Delta_R = \alpha \Delta_S + (1 - \alpha) \Delta_{\text{cash}}$$
$$= \alpha.$$

The delta of the security is 1, and the delta of the cash equivalent (relative to the underlying security) is zero. Consequently, the delta of the replicating portfolio is equal to alpha, or the proportion of the replicating portfolio put in the underlying security.

To replicate the movement of the option, the investor sets the delta of the desired option equal to the delta of the replicating portfolio (which is equal to alpha). Therefore, the proportion invested in the underlying security is equal to the delta of the option to be replicated, and the remainder is invested in cash equivalents.

To illustrate the creation of a protective-put strategy on stocks, consider the price movement of the portfolio to be replicated as consisting of stock plus the put option ($V = S + P$). The delta of the desired portfolio is

$$\Delta_V = 1 + \Delta_p$$
$$= 1 + (\Delta_c - 1)$$
$$= \Delta_c,$$

that is, it is equal to the delta of the associated call option (because the delta of the put option can be expressed in terms of the call option). This portfolio is duplicated with stock and a riskless bond (cash):

$$R = \alpha S + (1 - \alpha) \text{ cash}$$
$$\Delta_R = \alpha.$$

To replicate the price movement of the target strategy, the deltas are set equal to each other:

$$\Delta_V = \Delta_R$$
$$\Delta_c = \alpha,$$

that is, the investor sets the proportion of stock in the replicating portfolio equal to the delta of a call option with exercise price and time to maturity the same as the desired put option. The delta of a call option ranges from 0 to 1, so the proportion of the risky security in the replicating portfolio also ranges from 0 to 1 as prices fluctuate.

Table 6.7 provides an example of a protective put. As the security price goes up, the delta of the call option increases, and the investor increases the percentage of the security in the portfolio. As prices fall, the delta of the call option decreases, which requires a decrease in the proportion of the security in the portfolio. Because the delta of a call option is not a constant as the price moves, the investor has to alter the mix of the risky security in the portfolio to match the delta of the call option.

Table 6.7 Protective Put Replication

Security Price	Proportion in the Security ($\alpha = \Delta_c$)
$120	0.88
110	0.78
100	0.63
90	0.44
80	0.25
70	0.01

Note: $S_0 = E = \$100$, $r = 5\%$, $T = 1$ year, $\sigma = 22\%$.

Another example of dynamic option creation is the replication of a covered-call strategy ($V = S - C$). The delta of the covered-call portfolio is

$$\Delta_V = 1 - \Delta_c.$$

The replicating portfolio of stocks and cash is the same as the one used in the protective-put example [$R = \alpha S + (1 - \alpha)$Cash; $\Delta_R = \alpha$]. To replicate the covered-call strategy, the deltas are set equal so that the proportion of stock in the portfolio is equal to

$$\Delta_V = 1 - \Delta_c$$

$$= \alpha.$$

As the security price moves, the proportion in the security has to change in order to create the covered-call effect. An example of this strategy is shown in Table 6.8.

Table 6.8 Covered Call Replication

Security Price	Proportion in the Security ($1 - \Delta_c = \alpha$)
$120	0.12
110	0.22
100	0.37
90	0.56
80	0.75
70	0.99

Note: $S_0 = E = \$100$, $r = 5\%$, $T = 1$ year, $\sigma = 22\%$.

In the dynamic option creation approach, an investor can transfer funds in the portfolio between the security and cash in appropriate amounts, and the portfolio will behave as if a put option were purchased on the security itself. Because buying and selling the actual security is expensive, however, investors have tended to substitute futures contracts for the underlying security, which reduces transaction costs and speeds execution. Using futures has thus become a popular way of implementing portfolio insurance in recent years.

One other technique used to create optionlike effects is the replication of a long-term option using short-term options. Suppose an investor wants to buy a long-term option, but it is unavailable or very expensive. How could the investor create the effect of a long-term option by using available short-term options? Shown below is a value matrix using cash and two short-term options with different strike prices. The investor puts some money in a riskless bond (cash). He also buys w_1 units of a call option for which the exercise price is E_1, and w_2 units of a call option for which the exercise price is E_2. If the security price is below exercise price E_1 at the expiration

	$S < E_1$	$E_1 < S < E_2$	$S > E_2$
Cash (C)	$C(1 + rT)$	$C(1 + rT)$	$C(1 + rT)$
w_1 Call$_1$	0	$w_1(S - E_1)$	$w_1(S - E_1)$
w_2 Call$_2$	0	0	$w_2(S - E_2)$
Total payoff	$C(1 + rT)$	$C(1 + rT)$ $+ w_1(S - E_1)$	$C(1 + rT) + (w_1 + w_2)S$ $- w_1E_1 - w_2E_2$

of the short-term options, the strategy returns the bond principal plus the interest it has earned. If the security price is between E_1 and E_2, the strategy gives the bond payoff plus the payoff from the first option. If the security price is above E_2, the strategy gives the payoff on the bond, plus the payoff from both options.

Figure 6.11 illustrates this payoff pattern graphically. If the investor chooses the options carefully with the appropriate weights, he can approximately replicate the value of the long-term option at the expiration of the short-term options. At the expiration of the short-term options, the investor has approximately the same amount of money as the value of the long-term option. This value can then be reinvested in another series of short-term options to recreate the next period's value of the long-term option. Consequently, the investor can move step by step through time recreating the value of the longer term option until the expiration of the long-term option is reached. (See Choice and Novomestky 1989.)

Conclusion

Many similarities exist between using options and futures in managing the risk of investment positions and in creating market exposure synthetically. The fundamental hedging principles are the same whether dealing with options or futures

Figure 6.11 Replication of a Long-Term Option Using Short-Term Options

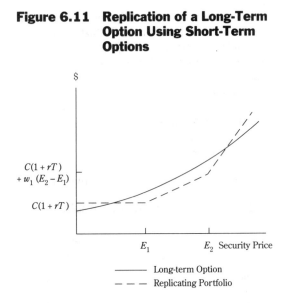

contracts. The asymmetry of options creates special problems in maintaining the stability of a hedge position, but it also creates important opportunities not generally available with futures contracts. This distinction is sometimes blurred, however, because dynamic trading strategies allow futures to replicate optionlike effects in a portfolio. All in all, the use of options and futures contracts gives investors an important tool for managing investment risk and creating desirable return patterns.

Exercises for Futures and Options

Futures Pricing

Exercise 1: Calculate the fair value of the following contracts with 45 days to expiration and an annualized interest rate of 7.3 percent for the 45-day period:

a. An equity index future with the current index level equal to 365.10 and the expected dividends until expiration equal to 1.60.

b. A foreign exchange future for British pounds with the current spot price equal to $1.850/pound and the 45-day foreign interest rate equal to 11.2 percent.

c. A Eurodollar future with the 90-day rate 45 days forward equal to 7.45 percent.

d. A Eurodollar future if the current Eurodollar rates for a 45-day maturity and a 135-day maturity are 7.30 percent and 7.69 percent, respectively. Note: to obtain the resulting fair futures price, calculate the implied 90-day rate 45 days forward.

e. A Treasury bond futures contract with the market price of the cheapest-to-deliver (CTD) bond equal to $74^{16}/_{32}$. The bond has a coupon rate of 7.25 percent, 16 days of accrued interest, and a delivery factor of 0.9194.

Solutions:

a. The fair value of the equity future is

$$F = S\left(1 + \frac{rt}{360}\right) - D = 365.10\left[1 + 0.073\left(\frac{45}{360}\right)\right] - 1.60 = 366.83.$$

b. The fair value for the foreign exchange future is

$$F = \frac{S\left(1 + \frac{r_d t}{360}\right)}{\left(1 + \frac{r_f t}{360}\right)} = 1.850 \frac{\left[1 + 0.073\left(\frac{45}{360}\right)\right]}{\left[1 + 0.112\left(\frac{45}{360}\right)\right]} = \$1.841/\text{pound}.$$

c. The fair value of the Eurodollar future is quoted as

$$F = 100(1 - f_{45}) = 100(1 - 0.0745) = 92.55.$$

d. The relationship between the current rates and the implied forward rate expressed as a money-market yield is

$$\left(1 + \frac{r_2 t_2}{360}\right) = \left(1 + \frac{r_1 t_1}{360}\right)\left(1 + \frac{{_1}f_2(t_2 - t_1)}{360}\right).$$

Solving for the implied forward rate gives

$$
{_1}f_2 = \left[\frac{\left(1 + \dfrac{r_2 t_2}{360}\right)}{\left(1 + \dfrac{r_1 t_1}{360}\right)} - 1\right]\frac{360}{(t_2 - t_1)} = \left[\frac{1 + 0.0769\left(\dfrac{135}{360}\right)}{1 + 0.073\left(\dfrac{45}{360}\right)} - 1\right]\frac{360}{(135 - 45)} = 7.81 \text{ percent.}
$$

The fair futures price is

$$F = 100(1 - {_1}f_2) = 100(1 - 0.0781) = 92.19.$$

e. The accrued interest on the bond is equal to

$$\frac{Bca}{365} = \frac{100(0.0725)(16)}{365} = 0.3178.$$

The price of the bond including accrued interest is

$$P = 74.5 + 0.3178 = 74.8178.$$

Using this price to calculate the price of the futures contract gives

$$
F = \left[\frac{P\left(1 + \dfrac{rt}{360}\right) - Bc\left(\dfrac{t+a}{365}\right)}{f}\right] = \frac{74.84\left[1 + 0.073\left(\dfrac{45}{360}\right)\right] - \dfrac{100(0.0725)(45 + 16)}{365}}{0.9194}
$$

$$= 80.825.$$

Implied Repo Rates

Exercise 2: If the actual price of the equity future in Exercise 1.a were 368.10, calculate the implied repo rate. How would an investor construct an arbitrage position to earn this rate of return?

Solution: The repo rate implied by the futures contract is

$$r = \left(\frac{F + D}{S} - 1\right)\frac{360}{t} = \left(\frac{368.10 + 1.60}{365.10} - 1\right)\frac{360}{45} = 10.08 \text{ percent.}$$

The arbitrage position would require buying a basket of stocks to replicate the S&P 500 Index and selling the futures contract. At the expiration of the contract in 45 days, the investor would have earned 10.08 percent annualized less any transaction costs to construct the portfolio. Any tracking error between the physical stocks and the index would add some variability to the arbitrage return.

Exercise 3: Calculate the implied domestic repo rate if the futures price in Exercise 1.b were equal to $1.854/pound. What arbitrage positions would create this rate of return?

Solution: The implied domestic repo rate can be found by rewriting the fair value relationship as

$$r_d = \left[\frac{F\left(1 + \frac{r_f t}{360}\right)}{S} - 1 \right] \frac{360}{t} = \left(\frac{1.854}{1.850} \left[1 + 0.112 \left(\frac{45}{360} \right) \right] - 1 \right) \frac{360}{45} = 12.95 \text{ percent.}$$

To capture this return, the investor has to convert dollars to pounds at the current exchange rate of $1.850/pound, invest at the foreign interest rate of 11.2 percent, and sell the futures contract. When the principal and interest in pounds are converted back into dollars and combined with the gains or losses on the futures contract, the realized dollar return on the strategy is 12.95 percent annualized less any transaction costs.

Basis and Calendar Spreads

Exercise 4: If the current S&P 500 Index were equal to 325.15 and 10 days later were equal to 324.10, and the nearby futures were equal to 327.05 and 326.25, respectively, calculate the basis at each date.

Solution: Common practice is to calculate the basis for the S&P 500 contract as the futures price minus the spot price so that the basis is a positive number. The basis at each point then would be

	Futures Price	Index Price	Basis
Current date	327.05	325.15	1.90
10 days later	326.25	324.10	2.15

Exercise 5: If the next maturity S&P 500 future in Exercise 4 were equal to 329.25 and 328.80, respectively, calculate the calendar spread at each date.

Solution: The calendar spread is commonly calculated for the S&P 500 by subtracting the nearby contract price from that of the deferred contract, so the spread generally results in a positive number:

	Deferred Contract	Nearby Contract	Calendar Spread
Current date	329.25	327.05	2.20
10 days later	328.80	326.25	2.55

Hedging Relationships

Exercise 6: Suppose an investor will receive a payment of 625 million yen in 30 days as a Japanese bond position matures but is concerned that the yen will depreciate relative to the dollar from its current level of $0.0071/yen.
a. Construct a simple hedge using the yen futures contract priced now at $0.0069/yen. How many contracts would need to be used?
b. If the spot exchange rate subsequently declines to $0.0067/yen and the futures price declines to $0.0066/yen, what is the net result of the hedge for the investor?
Solutions:
a. If the dollar value of the yen falls, the anticipated payment in yen will be worth less in dollars in 30 days than it is now. To hedge this decline in value, the investor would need to sell 50 futures contracts:

$$\frac{625,000,000 \text{ yen}}{12,500,000 \text{ yen/contract}} = 50 \text{ contracts.}$$

71

b. The value in dollars of 625 million yen sold forward is 0.0069($/yen) × 625 million yen = $4.3125 million. The actual value 30 days hence would be

	Exchange Rate ($/yen)	Yen Value	Dollar Value
Now + 30 days	0.0067	625M	$4.1875M
Gain from short futures position	(0.0069 − 0.0066)	625M	0.1875M
Net hedged value			$4.3750M

The value of the original forward commitment would be the same as the net hedged value if the basis had closed to zero at the termination of the hedge.

To see this perspective, write the net value from the hedge as the value of the terminal yen position times the net price created by the hedge

Net value = Yen value × $[F + (S_t - F_t)] = 625,000,000[0.0069 + (0.0067 - 0.0066)]$

$$= \$4,375,000.$$

The net value differs from the forward commitment by the amount of the basis at termination of the hedge.

Exercise 7: Using the following cash and futures prices, calculate the effect of a Eurodollar hedge constructed using a stack compared with one using a strip. What net advantage has been created using the strip?

	Now	Forward Roll Date (t)	Hedge Termination Date (T)
Spot index	93.85	92.55	92.50
Nearby contract (F^1)	92.50	92.45	—
Deferred contract (F^2)	92.25	92.25	92.20

Solution: The net price of the hedge created using a stack is

Net price (stack) = $S_T - (F_T^2 - F^2) = 92.50 - (92.20 - 92.25) = 92.55.$

The net price of the hedge created using a strip would be

Net price (strip) = $S_T - (F_t^1 - F^1) - (F_T^2 - F_t^2)$

$$= 92.50 - (92.45 - 92.50) - (92.20 - 92.25) = 92.60.$$

The difference between the net price of the stack and that of the strip is caused by the change in the calendar spread at the point of the roll (time t) versus the initiation of the hedge:

Net price (stack) − Net price (strip) = $(F_t^1 - F_t^2) - (F^1 - F^2)$

$$= (92.45 - 92.25) - (92.50 - 92.25) = -0.05.$$

Interest Rate Concepts

Exercise 8: Suppose the simple interest rate or money-market yield is 7 percent for 30 days. Convert this rate to a bank discount rate, an effective annual rate, a bond-equivalent yield, and a continuously compounded rate.

Solution: The relationship between a money-market yield and a bank discount rate is

$$d = \frac{r}{1 + \dfrac{rt}{360}} = \frac{0.07}{1 + 0.07\left(\dfrac{30}{360}\right)} = 6.96 \text{ percent.}$$

The effective annual rate is

$$i = \left(1 + \frac{rt}{360}\right)^{\frac{365}{t}} - 1 = \left[1 + 0.07\left(\frac{30}{360}\right)\right]^{\frac{365}{30}} - 1 = 7.33 \text{ percent.}$$

The bond-equivalent yield is

$$y = 2[(1 + i)^{1/2} - 1] = 2[(1.0733)^{1/2} - 1] = 7.20 \text{ percent.}$$

The continuously compounded rate is

$$c = \frac{ln(1 + i)}{T} = \frac{ln(1.0733)}{1.0} = 7.07 \text{ percent.}$$

Exercise 9: Calculate implied forward rates in the term structure if the current term structure is as follows:

Maturity (years)	Effective Annual Rate
1	$i_1 = 7.05$
2	$i_2 = 7.23$
3	$i_3 = 7.41$

Solution: The basic relationship between current and forward rates is given by

$$(1 + i_y)^y = (1 + i_x)(1 + {}_x f_y)^{y-x}.$$

The one-year rate one year forward ($x = 1$ and $y = 2$) is

$${}_1 f_2 = \frac{(1 + i_2)^2}{(1 + i_1)} - 1 = \frac{(1.0723)^2}{(1.0705)} - 1 = 7.41 \text{ percent.}$$

The one-year rate two years forward ($x = 2$ and $y = 3$) is

$${}_2 f_3 = \frac{(1 + i_3)^3}{(1 + i_2)^2} - 1 = \frac{(1.0741)^3}{(1.0723)^2} - 1 = 7.77 \text{ percent.}$$

The two-year rate one year forward ($x = 1$ and $y = 3$) is

$${}_1 f_3 = \left[\frac{(1 + i_3)^3}{(1 + i_1)}\right]^{1/2} - 1 = \left[\frac{(1.0741)^3}{(1.0705)}\right]^{1/2} - 1 = 7.59 \text{ percent.}$$

Exercise 10: Suppose the 90-day rate 45 days forward given by the Eurodollar future is equal to 8.05 percent. If the current 45-day rate and the 135-day rate were equal to 7.30 percent and 7.81 percent, respectively, what would be the implied forward rate in the current term structure? How could the futures contract be used to increase returns above those available in the current term structure?

Solution: The implied forward rate in the current term structure expressed as a money-market yield is

$${}_1 f_2 = \left[\frac{\left(1 + \dfrac{r_2 t_2}{360}\right)}{\left(1 + \dfrac{r_1 t_1}{360}\right)} - 1\right]\frac{360}{(t_2 - t_1)} = \left(\frac{\left[1 + 0.0781\left(\dfrac{135}{360}\right)\right]}{\left[1 + 0.0730\left(\dfrac{45}{360}\right)\right]} - 1\right)\frac{360}{(135 - 45)} = 7.99 \text{ percent.}$$

Because this forward rate is lower than the 8.05 percent in the Eurodollar futures contract, the investor could earn a higher rate over 135 days by investing for 45 days at 7.30 percent and buying a futures contract. The effective rate for 135 days is

$$r_2 = \left(\left[1 + \frac{r_1 t_1}{360}\right]\left[1 + {}_1 f_2 \frac{(t_2 - t_1)}{360}\right] - 1\right)\frac{360}{t_2}$$

$$= \left(\left[1 + 0.073\left(\frac{45}{360}\right)\right]\left[1 + 0.0805\left(\frac{90}{360}\right)\right] - 1\right)\frac{360}{135} = 7.85 \text{ percent.}$$

Duration and Convexity

Exercise 11: For the Treasury bond in Exercise 1.e, calculate the modified duration of the futures contract in the case of a parallel shift in the yield curve ($dr/dy = 1.0$). Assume that the Treasury bond has 25 years to maturity, pays interest semiannually, and has a 10.0 percent yield to maturity.

Solution: The modified duration of the Treasury bond in Exercise 1.e can be calculated as

$$D^* = \frac{B\left(c\left[1 + \frac{y}{2}\right]\left[\left(1 + \frac{y}{2}\right)^T - 1\right] + \frac{yT}{2}[y - c]\right)}{Py^2\left(1 + \frac{y}{2}\right)^{T+1}}$$

$$= \frac{100\left[0.0725(1.05)(1.05^{50} - 1) + \frac{0.10(50)}{2}(0.10 - 0.0725)\right]}{74.84(0.10)^2(1.05)^{51}} = 9.61 \text{ years.}$$

The modified duration of the futures contract can then be given as

$$D_F^* = \frac{P}{fF}\left[D^*\left(1 + \frac{rt}{360}\right) - (dr/dy)\left(\frac{t}{360}\right)\right]$$

$$= \frac{74.84}{0.9194(80.78)}\left(9.61\left[1 + 0.073\left(\frac{45}{360}\right)\right] - [1.0]\left[\frac{45}{360}\right]\right) = 9.65 \text{ years.}$$

Exercise 12: First, calculate the price, modified duration, and modified convexity of a bond paying interest semiannually with a 9.25 percent coupon, a yield to maturity of 8.50 percent, and a maturity of 10 years. Then, estimate the change in the price of the bond using its duration and convexity if its yield to maturity falls by 0.2 percent. How does this estimated price change compare with the actual price change?

Solution: The price of the bond can be found as

$$P = \frac{B\left(c\left[\left(1 + \frac{y}{2}\right)^T - 1\right] + y\right)}{y\left(1 + \frac{y}{2}\right)^T} = \frac{100(0.0925[(1.0425)^{20} - 1] + 0.085)}{(0.085)(1.0425)^{20}} = 104.99.$$

The modified duration is

$$D^* = \frac{B\left(c\left[1+\dfrac{y}{2}\right]\left[\left(1+\dfrac{y}{2}\right)^T - 1\right] + \dfrac{yT}{2}(y-c)\right)}{Py^2\left(1+\dfrac{y}{2}\right)^{T+1}}$$

$$= \frac{100\left(0.0925[1.0425][(1.0425)^{20} - 1] + \dfrac{0.085(20)}{2}[0.085 - 0.0925]\right)}{104.99(0.085)^2(1.0425)^{21}}$$

$$= 6.54 \text{ years.}$$

The modified convexity of the bond is

$$C^* = \frac{B\left(2c\left[1+\dfrac{y}{2}\right]^2\left[\left(1+\dfrac{y}{2}\right)^{T-1} - 1\right] - cyT\left[1+\dfrac{y}{2}\right] + y^2 T[T+1]\dfrac{[y-c]}{4}\right)}{Py^3\left(1+\dfrac{y}{2}\right)^{T+2}}$$

$$= \frac{100\left(2[0.0925][1.0425]^2[(1.0425)^{19} - 1] - 0.0925[0.085][20][1.0425] + [0.085]^2[20][21]\dfrac{[0.085 - 0.0925]}{4}\right)}{104.99(0.085)^3(1.0425)^{22}}$$

$$= 45.13.$$

The estimated change in the price of the bond if interest rates fall by 0.2 percent is

$$\Delta P = P\left[-D^*\Delta y + \frac{C^*}{2}(\Delta y)^2\right] = 104.99\left[-6.54(-0.002) + \frac{45.13}{2}(-0.002)^2\right]$$

$$= \$1.38.$$

The actual price of the bond if rates fall to 8.3 percent is

$$P = \frac{B\left(c\left[\left(1+\dfrac{y}{2}\right)^T - 1\right] + y\right)}{y\left(1+\dfrac{y}{2}\right)^T} = \frac{100[0.0925(1.0415^{20} - 1) + 0.083]}{0.083(1.0415)^{20}} = \$106.37.$$

The actual change in price would be $106.37 - $104.99 = $1.38, compared with the estimate of $1.38 using the duration and convexity measures. The change in yield to maturity of 0.2 percent is small enough so that the estimated price change is a close approximation to the actual change.

Hedge Positions

Exercise 13: Calculate a delta-neutral hedge ratio and the number of contracts required to hedge the positions described below. Assume that the futures contracts expire in 30 days and that the current 30-day interest rate is equal to 8.0 percent:

a. Hedge a $50 million equity portfolio that has a beta of 0.98 relative to the S&P 500 Index, which is at 350. How would the hedge positions differ if the contracts expired in three days?

b. Hedge a £50 million exposure with the 30-day U.K. interest rate at 10.6 percent.

c. Hedge a $50 million (face value) Treasury bill position, assuming that the cash and futures discount rates move one to one. Also assume that the Treasury bill matures in 90 days. What would the hedge positions be for bills expiring in 120 days?

d. Hedge the interest rate on a 180-day loan for $50 million. Assume that the interest rate on the loan is correlated one to one with the Eurodollar rate.

e. Hedge a $50 million (market value) corporate bond position with a Treasury bond futures position. Assume that corporate yields will change by 12 basis points when Treasury bond rates change by 10 basis points. The modified duration for the corporate bond position is 6.3 years and the modified duration for the future is 8.7 years. The average price of the corporate bond is $89^{12}/_{32}$, and the future is priced at $92^{16}/_{32}$. Assume the price of the CTD Treasury bond is equal to $94^{18}/_{32}$.

Solutions:

a. The hedge ratio for the equity portfolio is

$$h = \frac{-\beta}{\left(1 + \dfrac{rt}{360}\right)} = \frac{-0.98}{\left[1 + .08\left(\dfrac{30}{360}\right)\right]} = -0.974.$$

The number of contracts required is

$$n = \frac{h \times \text{Portfolio value}}{\text{Contract size}} = \frac{-0.974(50,000,000)}{350(500)} = -278 \text{ contracts.}$$

If the contracts expire in three days, the hedge ratio is

$$h = \frac{-0.98}{\left[1 + 0.08\left(\dfrac{3}{360}\right)\right]} = -0.98.$$

The number of contracts would be altered slightly, giving

$$n = \frac{-0.98(50,000,000)}{350(500)} = -280 \text{ contracts.}$$

Fewer contracts are required when the futures have a longer expiration because a change in the index produces a slightly larger change in the futures price; that is,

$$\Delta F = \Delta I\left(1 + \frac{rt}{360}\right).$$

The closer the expiration date of the futures contract, the more the future moves one to one with the index.

b. The hedge ratio for the British pound exposure is

$$h = \frac{-\left(1 + \dfrac{r_f t}{360}\right)}{\left(1 + \dfrac{r_d t}{360}\right)} = \frac{-\left[1 + 0.106\left(\dfrac{30}{360}\right)\right]}{\left[1 + 0.08\left(\dfrac{30}{360}\right)\right]} = -1.0022.$$

In many applications, the interest rate differentials are not large enough to drive the hedge ratio far from 1. As a result, most investors use 1 as the typical hedge ratio in foreign exchange hedging. The number of contracts required is

$$n = \frac{h \times \text{Hedge value}}{\text{Contract size}} = \frac{-1.0022(50,000,000)}{62,500} = -802 \text{ contracts.}$$

c. The hedge ratio for the Treasury bill position is

$$h = \frac{\left(\dfrac{-t}{360}\right)}{0.25}\left(\frac{\Delta d}{\Delta d_f}\right) = \frac{\left(\dfrac{-90}{360}\right)}{0.25}(1.0) = -1.0.$$

The number of contracts is

$$n = \frac{h \times \text{Hedge value}}{\text{Contract size}} = \frac{-1.0(50,000,000)}{1,000,000} = -50 \text{ contracts.}$$

If the bills expire in 120 days, the hedge ratio is

$$h = \frac{\left(\dfrac{-120}{360}\right)}{0.25}(1.0) = -1.333.$$

The hedge ratio is greater in this case because the bills have a longer maturity than those underlying the futures contract and will change more in price for a given change in the discount rate. The number of contracts required is

$$n = \frac{-1.333(50,000,000)}{1,000,000} = -67 \text{ contracts.}$$

d. The hedge ratio for the interest rate on the loan is

$$h = \frac{\left(\dfrac{-t}{360}\right)}{0.25\left(1 + \dfrac{rt}{360}\right)}\left(\frac{\Delta r}{\Delta r_f}\right) = \frac{\left(\dfrac{-180}{360}\right)}{0.25\left[1 + 0.08\left(\dfrac{180}{360}\right)\right]}(1.0) = -1.923.$$

Each contract represents the interest earned on $1 million for three months. For a six-month loan, generally two contracts would be required for each $1 million of loan principal. The hedge ratio is slightly less than 2 because interest is paid at the end of the loan, but the gains from the hedge will occur 180 days earlier, when the rate is fixed. Consequently, the hedge ratio is adjusted by a present value factor for the difference in timing. The number of contracts required is

$$n = \frac{h \times \text{Loan value}}{\text{Contract size}} = \frac{-1.923(50,000,000)}{1,000,000} = -96 \text{ contracts.}$$

e. A cross hedge can be constructed for the corporate bond position with Treasury bond futures because changes in corporate and Treasury interest rates are correlated with each other. The expected ratio for a change in rates is

$$\frac{\Delta y_B}{\Delta y} = \frac{12\ bp}{10\ bp} = 1.2.$$

The hedge ratio for the portfolio is

$$h = \frac{-D^*B}{D_F^*F}\left(\frac{\Delta y_B}{\Delta y}\right) = \frac{-6.3(89.375)}{8.7(92.50)}(1.2) = -0.84.$$

The number of contracts required is

$$n = \frac{h \times \text{Portfolio value}}{\text{Contract size}} = \frac{0.84(50,000,000)}{94.5625(1,000)} = -444 \text{ contracts.}$$

Exercise 14: Suppose an investor has a portfolio with the following characteristics:

	Market Value	Current Portfolio Proportion	Risk Exposure
Bonds	$13,000,000	0.36	Duration = 7.2 years
Stocks	23,000,000	0.64	Beta = 0.93
Total	$36,000,000	1.00	

but desires a portfolio with the following characteristics:

	Market Value	Desired Portfolio Proportion	Risk Exposure
Bonds	$16,200,000	0.45	Duration = 8.3 years
Stocks	19,800,000	0.55	Beta = 1.0
Total	$36,000,000	1.00	

What hedge ratios would be required and how many futures contracts would be needed to achieve the desired proportions? Assume that the duration of the Treasury bond contract is equal to 8.9 years and the futures contracts expire in 50 days. Also assume that the 50-day interest rate is equal to 7.5 percent, the S&P 500 Index is at 360.05, and the Treasury bond futures contract is priced at 95 16/32 with the underlying bonds in the portfolio priced at 87 24/32. In addition, assume that the estimated relative change in yield to maturity between the bond portfolio and the CTD bond is 1.0, with the CTD bond priced at 95 9/32.

Solution: The hedge ratio for the desired equity exposure is

$$h_E = \frac{\theta_V^E \beta_V - \theta_S \beta_S}{\left(1 + \frac{rt}{360}\right)} = \frac{0.55(1.0) - 0.64(0.93)}{\left[1 + 0.075\left(\frac{50}{360}\right)\right]} = -0.045.$$

The required number of equity futures contracts is

$$n_E = \frac{h_E\ \theta_V^E\ (\text{Total portfolio value})}{\text{Contract size}} = \frac{-0.045(0.55)\ (36,000,000)}{360.05(500)} = -5 \text{ contracts.}$$

The hedge ratio for the desired bond exposure is

$$h_B = \frac{B(\theta_V^B D_V^* - \theta_B D_B^*)}{D_F^* F} \left(\frac{\Delta y_B}{\Delta y} \right) = \frac{87.75[0.45(8.3) - 0.36(7.2)]}{8.9(95.5)} (1.0) = 0.118.$$

The required number of bond contracts is

$$n_B = \frac{h_B \; \theta_V^B \; \text{(Total portfolio value)}}{\text{Contract size}} = \frac{0.118(0.45) \; (36,000,000)}{95.25(1,000)} (1.0) = 20 \text{ contracts.}$$

Risk/Return Characteristics of Options

Exercise 15: To illustrate the principles applied in analyzing payoff patterns beyond the discussion in Chapter 4, this exercise considers several additional strategies. Prepare the value matrix and the payoff profile for each of the following strategies:

a. *Short straddle.* Sell a put and a call with the same strike price.
b. *Bear put spread.* Buy a put at strike price E_2, and sell a put at strike price E_1 ($E_2 > E_1$).
c. *Butterfly spread.* Buy two different call options at strike prices E_3 and E_1, and sell two call options at the same strike price E_2 ($E_3 > E_2 > E_1$).
d. *Strangle.* Buy a put option with strike price E_1, and buy a call option with strike price E_2 ($E_1 < E_2$).
e. *Ratio spread.* Buy a call option at strike price E_1, and sell two call options at strike price E_2 ($E_1 < E_2$).
f. *Condor.* Sell two different call options at strike prices E_2 and E_3, and buy two different call options at strike prices E_1 and E_4 ($E_1 < E_2 < E_3 < E_4$).
g. *Box spread.* Buy a call option with strike price E_1, and sell a call option with strike price E_2. In addition, sell a put option at strike price E_2, and buy a put option at strike price E_1 ($E_1 < E_2$).

Solutions:

a. The short straddle is constructed by selling a put and a call option with the same strike price. The value matrix is

	$S < E$	$S > E$
−Call	0	$-(S - E)$
−Put	$-(E - S)$	0
Payoff	$S - E$	$E - S$

Plotting that payoff structure results in the configuration in Figure E-1. The short-straddle position yields a positive net profit as long as the security stays close to the strike price. If the security moves away from the exercise price in either direction by more than the net option premiums, the short-straddle position shows a loss. The benefits from this strategy occur if the security price does not swing widely; the risks can be sizable for large moves in the security price.

b. The bear put spread is constructed by buying a put option at a high strike price E_2 and selling a put option at a lower strike price E_1. The value matrix is

	$S < E_1$	$E_1 < S < E_2$	$S > E_2$
+ Put$_2$	$E_2 - S$	$E_2 - S$	0
− Put$_1$	$-(E_1 - S)$	0	0
Payoff	$E_2 - E_1$	$E_2 - S$	0

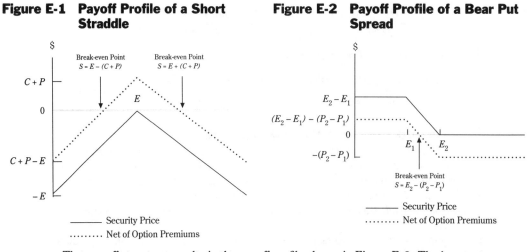

Figure E-1   Payoff Profile of a Short Straddle

Figure E-2   Payoff Profile of a Bear Put Spread

That payoff structure results in the payoff profile shown in Figure E-2. The bear put spread yields a positive payoff if the security price drops below the break-even point. The benefits of this strategy occur for the investor with a bearish outlook for the security. Both the potential gains and losses are limited.

c. The butterfly spread is created by buying two call options with separate strike prices and selling two call options with a strike price between those of the two long call positions. The value matrix is

	$S < E_1$	$E_1 < S < E_2$	$E_2 < S < E_3$	$S > E_3$
$+\text{Call}_1$	0	$S - E_1$	$S - E_1$	$S - E_1$
$+\text{Call}_3$	0	0	0	$S - E_3$
-2Calls_2	0	0	$-2(S - E_2)$	$-2(S - E_2)$
Payoff	0	$S - E_1$	$2E_2 - S - E_1$	$2E_2 - E_1 - E_3$

The payoff profile for this matrix is shown in Figure E-3. If the strike prices are equally spaced, the payoff profile on the upside is zero like that on the downside before the option premiums are taken into account. The benefits of this strategy occur if the security price stays close to the middle strike price E_2. The risk is limited on the downside, however. This strategy results in negative net profits as the security price approaches or exceeds the outside strike prices.

d. The strangle is constructed by buying a put option and a call option with different strike prices. The strike price of the put option should be lower than that of the call option. The value matrix is

	$S < E_1$	$E_1 < S < E_2$	$S > E_2$
Call_2	0	0	$S - E_2$
Put_1	$E_1 - S$	0	0
Payoff	$E_1 - S$	0	$S - E_2$

The payoff profile is shown in Figure E-4. The strangle generates positive net profits out beyond the options' exercise prices. If the security price stays within the break-even points, however, the investor receives a negative payoff.

e. The upside ratio spread is constructed by buying a call option at a low strike price and selling two call options at higher strike prices. The value matrix is

Figure E-3   Payoff Profile of a Butterfly Spread

Figure E-4   Payoff Profile of a Strangle

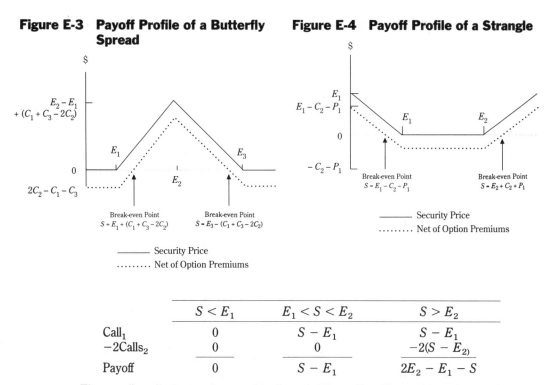

	$S < E_1$	$E_1 < S < E_2$	$S > E_2$
Call$_1$	0	$S - E_1$	$S - E_1$
-2Calls$_2$	0	0	$-2(S - E_2)$
Payoff	0	$S - E_1$	$2E_2 - E_1 - S$

The payoff profile for a ratio spread is shown in Figure E-5. The upside ratio spread would give positive net profits so long as the security price remains less than the break-even point. Beyond that point, the risk of loss is magnified somewhat because the two short-call options' positions lose $2.00 for every $1.00 increase in the security price. A ratio spread on the downside could also be constructed by purchasing one put and selling two others at lower strike prices.

f. The condor is constructed by selling two call options with separate strike prices near the money and buying two additional call options with strike prices outside the two short positions. The condor is similar to the butterfly spread except that the two short call positions have different strike prices. The value matrix is

Figure E-5   Payoff Profile of a Ratio Spread

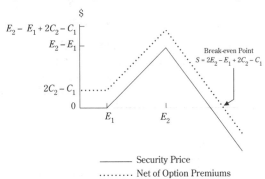

Figure E-6 Payoff Profile of a Condor

Figure E-7 Payoff Profile of a Box Spread

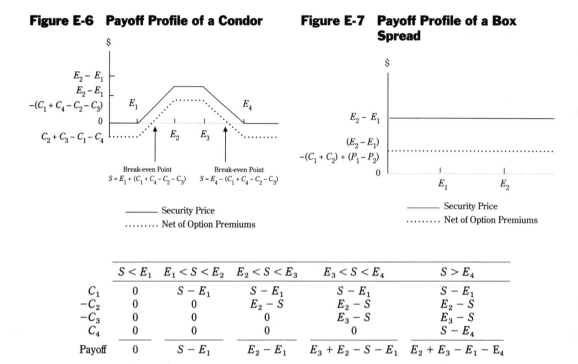

	$S < E_1$	$E_1 < S < E_2$	$E_2 < S < E_3$	$E_3 < S < E_4$	$S > E_4$
C_1	0	$S - E_1$	$S - E_1$	$S - E_1$	$S - E_1$
$-C_2$	0	0	$E_2 - S$	$E_2 - S$	$E_2 - S$
$-C_3$	0	0	0	$E_3 - S$	$E_3 - S$
C_4	0	0	0	0	$S - E_4$
Payoff	0	$S - E_1$	$E_2 - E_1$	$E_3 + E_2 - S - E_1$	$E_2 + E_3 - E_1 - E_4$

The payoff profile would be as shown in Figure E-6. If the strike prices are equally spaced, the payoff profile on the upside will give a 0 value like that on the downside before the option premiums are taken into account. The benefits of the strategy occur if the security price stays between the break-even points. Outside that range, the strategy will generate negative net profits. Unlike the short straddle, however, the condor's losses are limited.

g. The box spread is really a spread of two spreads. It is constructed by buying a bull call spread and selling a bull put spread. The pair of option strike prices for the put and call spreads are the same, with E_2 greater than E_1. The value matrix is

	$S < E_1$	$E_1 < S < E_2$	$S > E_2$
$+\text{Call}_1$	0	$S - E_1$	$S - E_1$
$-\text{Call}_2$	0	0	$-(S - E_2)$
$-\text{Put}_1$	$-(E_1 - S)$	0	0
$+\text{Put}_2$	$E_2 - S$	$E_2 - S$	0
Payoff	$E_2 - E_1$	$E_2 - E_1$	$E_2 - E_1$

The payoff profile for the box spread, shown in Figure E-7, creates a riskless profile: The payoff is constant no matter what happens to the security price. Because the payoff is constant, the options should be priced to give a net payoff equal to the riskless interest rate. Otherwise, a riskless arbitrage could be constructed to yield greater than riskless returns with no risk to the investor.

Performance Analysis

Exercise 16: Consider the two probability distributions of returns from two different covered-call strategies on the market index with a one-year horizon as shown

Table E-1 Return Probabilities: Two Covered-Call Strategies

Return Range	Option Strategy $(r^E = 0.0\%)$	Option Strategy $(r^E = 15.0\%)$	Market Index
Below −15%	2.2	4.3	6.7
−15 to −5	4.3	6.9	9.2
−5 to 5	9.0	12.5	15.0
5 to 15	84.5	17.7	19.1
15 to 25	0.0	58.6	19.1
25 to 35	0.0	0.0	15.0
Above 35	0.0	0.0	15.9
Total	100.0	100.0	100.0
Average return $(\overline{R})$	10.0%	12.8%	15.0%
Standard deviation (σ)	7.6%	12.7%	20.0%
Average beta (β)	0.27	0.56	1.0
Option security price	9.7%	4.0%	—
Skewness	−2.8	−1.4	0.0

in Table E-1. The first uses index options that are at the money. The second uses options that are 15 percent out of the money. Compare the risk/return relationships of these two strategies. Assume a riskless rate of 7.0 percent. What are the trade-offs in choosing one strategy over another?

Solution: Using the standard measures for comparing risk and return for symmetric return distributions gives the results shown in Table E-2.

The covered-call strategy with at-the-money options offers better risk-adjusted returns when using the Treynor ratio and the measure of total return per standard deviation. The Sharpe ratio suggests that the covered-call strategy using out-of-the-money options is somewhat the better strategy. By these measures, both covered-call strategies are generally better than just holding the market index alone.

A comparison of the return-range probabilities shows that both option strategies cut off the possibility of high returns and increase the probability of moderate returns. The higher the strike price on the call option, the less distortion the option strategy creates in the return distribution relative to the market index. This effect is borne out by the

Table E-2 Return Results: Two Covered-Call Strategies

Measure	Option Strategy $r^E = 0.0\%$	Option Strategy $r^E = 15.0\%$	Market Index
$\overline{R}/\sigma$	$\dfrac{10.0}{7.6} = 1.32$	$\dfrac{12.8}{12.7} = 1.01$	$\dfrac{15.0}{20.0} = 0.75$
Sharpe Ratio: $\dfrac{\overline{R} - R_f}{\sigma}$	$\dfrac{10.0 - 7.0}{7.6} = 0.39$	$\dfrac{12.8 - 7.0}{12.7} = 0.46$	$\dfrac{15.0 - 7.0}{20.0} = 0.40$
Treynor Ratio: $\dfrac{\overline{R} - R_f}{\beta}$	$\dfrac{10.0 - 7.0}{0.27} = 11.11$	$\dfrac{12.8 - 7.0}{0.56} = 10.36$	$\dfrac{15.0 - 7.0}{1.0} = 8.00$

skewness, average beta, and standard deviation of each portfolio. The at-the-money options produce more distortion than those out of the money. Finally, the at-the-money options are more expensive, so they result in higher premiums received than the out-of-the-money options.

The data presented here provide little basis for choosing which strategy is best. A description of the impact of the different option strategies does not indicate which one a particular investor might prefer. In general, the covered-call strategy works best when option prices are expensive and expectations for the market are more neutral than bullish. If the investor has these expectations, the use of a covered-call strategy may be desirable. The choice of strike price is influenced by how strongly the expectations are held. High confidence in a neutral market allows the investor to sell at-the-money options comfortably, but an investor with less confidence may feel more comfortable selling out-of-the-money options.

Option Pricing

Exercise 17: Following the pattern used for the call option in Figure 4.1, derive the relationship of the put price to its adjusted intrinsic value.

Solution: The relationship can be found by creating a value matrix for the strategy that buys a put option and buys the security. Because the total payoff at each point is greater than or equal to the payoff from investing in the riskless discount bond, which has a payoff of E dollars, the present value of the bond must be less than or equal to that of the put option and the security:

$$\frac{E}{(1 + rT)} \le P + S_0,$$

or equivalently,

$$P \ge \frac{E}{(1 + rT)} - S_0.$$

For an American put option, which can be exercised early, the put option would be worth at least as much as its intrinsic value $E - S_0$. The European option, however, would only need to satisfy the less restrictive constraint by being greater than $E/(1 + rT) - S_0$.

Exercise 18: Using the binomial model, calculate the value of a call option with the following parameters:

$E = \$95$,
$S_0 = \$100$,
$S_u = \$115$,
$S_d = \$90$,
$r = 8.0$ percent/period, and
$t = 1$.

Solution: The parameters needed to price the call option using the binomial model are

$$q = \frac{S_0(1 + rt) - S_d}{S_u - S_d} = \frac{100(1.08) - 90}{115 - 90} = 0.72,$$

$$C_u = \max(0, S_u - E) = \max(0, 115 - 95) = 20, \text{ and}$$

$$C_d = \max(0, S_d - E) = \max(0, 90 - 95) = 0.$$

The value of the call option is

$$C = \frac{qC_u + (1-q)\,C_d}{(1+rt)} = \frac{0.72(20) + (0.28)0}{(1.08)} = \$13.33.$$

Exercise 19: Calculate the value of a put option using the same data as in Exercise 18.

Solution: The payoff from the put option is

$$P_u = \max(0,\ E - S_u) = \max(0,\ 95 - 115) = 0,\ \text{and}$$

$$P_d = \max(0,\ E - S_d) = \max(0,\ 95 - 90) = 5.$$

The value of the put option is

$$P = \frac{qP_u + (1-q)\,P_d}{1+rt} = \frac{0.72(0) + (0.28)5}{1.08} = \$1.30.$$

Exercise 20:

a. Using only stock and a riskless bond, create the same payoff as the call option in Exercise 18. How much in the riskless bond and how many shares of stock must be used to give the equivalent payoff for the call option?

b. What combinations of stock and a riskless bond would have to be used to recreate the payoff of the put option in Exercise 19?

Solutions:

a. The hedge ratio for the call option is given by:

$$h = \frac{-(S_u - S_d)}{(C_u - C_d)} = \frac{-(115 - 90)}{(20 - 0)} = -1.25.$$

The initial investment is

$$B_0 = S_0 + hC = 100 - 1.25(13.33) = \$83.34.$$

The call option expressed in terms of the beginning investment in a riskless bond and the stock is

$$C = \frac{B_0 - S_0}{h},$$

which implies that the payoff from the call option can be recreated by investing B_0/h in the riskless bond and $-S/h$ in stock. This combination implies

$$\frac{B_0}{h} = \frac{83.34}{-1.25} = -\$66.67,\ \text{and}$$

$$\frac{-S_0}{h} = \frac{-100}{-1.25} = \$80.00.$$

The payoff pattern from the call option can be recreated by borrowing $66.67 at 8 percent and investing a total of $80.00 in stock (0.8 shares). The net investment would be $80.00 - \$66.67 = \$13.33$, with the following payoff pattern:

Position	Stock Up		Stock Down	
0.8 stock	$0.8(115) =$	92	$0.8(90) =$	72
Bond	$-1.08(66.67) =$	-72	$-1.08(66.67) =$	-72
Net payoff		20		0

b. The hedge ratio for the put option is

$$h = \frac{-(S_u - S_d)}{(P_u - P_d)} = \frac{-(115 - 90)}{(0 - 5)} = 5.0.$$

The initial investment is given by

$$B_0 = S_0 + hP = 100 + 5(1.30) = \$106.50.$$

The put option expressed in terms of the stock and beginning investment in the riskless bond is

$$P = \frac{B_0 - S_0}{h}.$$

The investments in the bond and stock are

$$\frac{B_0}{h} = \frac{106.5}{5} = \$21.30, \text{ and}$$

$$\frac{-S_0}{h} = \frac{-100}{5} = -\$20.00.$$

To recreate the payoff pattern of the put option, the investor would short $20.00 of stock (0.2 shares) and invest $21.30 in a riskless bond at 8 percent.

Exercise 21:

a. Using the Black-Scholes model, calculate the value of a call option on a stock with the following parameters:

$S_0 = \$90,$
$E = \$95,$
$r = 8$ percent/year,
$T = 3/12$ year, and
$\sigma = 39.0$ percent.

b. Using the same parameters, calculate the price of the call option with one week left to expiration.

c. Calculate the price of a put option with the same parameters.

Solutions:

a. The parameters for the Black-Scholes model are

$$d_1 = \frac{\ln\left(\frac{S_0}{E}\right) + (r + \frac{1}{2}\sigma^2)T}{\sigma\sqrt{T}} = \frac{\ln\left[\frac{90}{95}\right] + [0.08 + \frac{1}{2}(0.39)^2]\frac{1}{4}}{0.39\sqrt{\frac{1}{4}}} = -0.0772,$$

$$d_2 = d_1 - \sigma\sqrt{T} = -0.2722,$$

$$N(d_1) = 0.4692, \text{ and}$$

$$N(d_2) = 0.3927.$$

The price of the call option is

$$C = S_0 N(d_1) - e^{-rT} EN(d_2) = 90(0.4692) - 0.980(95)(0.3927) = \$5.66.$$

b. With one week to expiration, the parameters are

$$d_1 = -0.9457,$$
$$d_2 = -0.9997,$$
$$N(d_1) = 0.1722,$$
$$N(d_2) = 0.1589, \text{ and}$$
$$C = 90(0.1722) - 0.998(95)(0.1589) = \$0.43.$$

c. The put/call parity relationship gives

$$P = Ee^{-rT} + C - S_0.$$

For the three-month option, the put price is

$$P = 95(0.980) + 5.66 - 90 = \$8.76.$$

For the one-week option, the put price is

$$P = 95(0.998) + 0.43 - 90 = \$5.24.$$

Exercise 22: Suppose a put option on a security has the parameters shown below. At what security price would exercising the put option early be desirable?

$$E = \$50,$$
$$r = 6.5 \text{ percent/year},$$
$$T = 1/6 \text{ year, and}$$
$$\sigma = 22.3 \text{ percent.}$$

Solution: As the security price drops from a level of $50, the price of a comparable call option would also fall. The early exercise point would occur when

$$C < \frac{ErT}{(1 + rT)} = 0.54, \text{ or}$$

$$P < E - S_0 .$$

The result is shown in Table E-3.

Table E-3 Early Exercise Point

Security Price (S_0)	Call Price (C)	Put Price (P)	$E - S_0$
$50	$2.06	$1.55	0.00
49	1.54	2.03	1.00
48	1.11	2.60	2.00
47	0.77	3.26	3.00
46[a]	0.51	4.00	4.00
45	0.32	4.81	5.00

[a]Early exercise would be desirable when the security price falls to approximately $46.

87

Exercise 23: Suppose a stock follows a two-period binomial process as shown in Figure E-8. Calculate the price of an American call option on this stock. The option has a strike price of $100, and the interest rate is 3.0 percent per period. Notice that the movements are not proportional up and down and that the stock pays dividends in Period 1. Also note that, if the stock price goes up, the stock will pay a dividend of $5 at the end of the first period. It will pay only $1 if the stock price goes down. Compare the price of the American option to that of a European option.

Figure E-8   A Two-Period Binomial Process

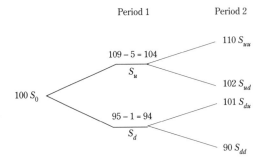

Solution: Finding the value for the European option requires finding the price of the option at each stage by working backward from Period 1 to the present. If the stock price rises in Period 1, the value of the European call option in Period 1 is

$$q_u = \frac{S_u(1 + rt) - S_{ud}}{S_{uu} - S_{ud}} = \frac{104(1.03) - 102}{110 - 102} = 0.64, \text{ and}$$

$$C_u = \frac{q_u C_{uu} + (1 - q_u)C_{ud}}{(1 + rt)} = \frac{0.64(10) + (1 - 0.64)(2)}{1.03} = \$6.91.$$

If the stock price falls in Period 1, the value of the European call option in Period 1 is

$$q_d = \frac{S_d(1 + rt) - S_{dd}}{S_{du} - S_{dd}} = \frac{94(1.03) - 90}{101 - 90} = 0.62, \text{ and}$$

$$C_d = \frac{q_d C_{du} + (1 - q_d) C_{dd}}{(1 + rt)} = \frac{0.62(1) - (1 - 0.62)0}{1.03} = \$0.60.$$

If the option were European without the possibility of early exercise, the value of the option at the beginning is

$$q = \frac{S_0 (1 + rt) - S_d}{S_u - S_d} = \frac{100(1.03) - 94}{1.04 - 94} = 0.90, \text{ and}$$

$$C = \frac{q C_u + (1 - q)C_d}{(1 + rt)} = \frac{0.90 (6.91) + (1 - 90)(0.60)}{1.03} = \$6.10.$$

If the option is American, however, a better strategy may be to exercise it immediately, before the stock goes ex-dividend in Period 1 and falls in price. If the stock price rises in Period 1, the value of the option if exercised in Period 1 is

$$C_u^* = (S_u + D_u) - E = (104 + 5) - 100 = \$9.00.$$

In this case, the exercised value of the option before the ex-dividend drop in stock price is larger than the $6.91 value of the call option after the dividend payment in Period 1. Exercising the option early would be better than holding it.

If the stock price falls in Period 1, the European option is worth $0.60. Early exercise of the call option would not be desirable because the option is out of the money and early exercise would cost $5:

$$(S_d + D_d) - E = (94 + 1) - 100 = -\$5.00.$$

Substituting the value of the exercised call option in Period 1 in place of the European price would give the initial value for the American call option:

$$C = \frac{q\,C_u^* + (1 - q)C_d}{(1 + r)} = \frac{0.90(9) + (1 - 0.90)\,(0.60)}{1.03} = \$7.92.$$

The ability to exercise the option early adds $1.82 to the value of the European call option and increases its price from $6.10 to $7.92.

Exercise 24:

a. Calculate the put and call option prices on a future with the following parameters:

E = $98,
F = $97.50,
r = 8 percent/year,
T = 30/365 year, and
σ = 20.0 percent.

b. If S_0 = $96, calculate the put and call option prices on the cash security with the same parameters. Should they be the same?

c. Using the same parameters, calculate the value of the futures contract at which early exercise might be desirable for the put and call futures options.

Solutions:

a. The values of the parameters for the Black model are

$$d_1 = \frac{\ln\left(\dfrac{F}{E}\right) + \tfrac{1}{2}\sigma^2 T}{\sigma\sqrt{T}} = 0.0601,$$

$$d_2 = d_1 - \sigma\,T = -0.1179,$$
$$N(d_1) = 0.4761, \text{ and}$$
$$N(d_2) = 0.4530.$$

Using these values gives the prices of the put and call futures options:

$$C = [FN(d_1) - EN(d_2)]e^{-rT} = \$2.01, \text{ and}$$
$$P = C + (E - F)e^{-rT} = \$2.51.$$

b. The values of the parameters for the Black-Scholes model are

$$d_1 = \frac{\ln\left(\dfrac{S_0}{E}\right) + (r + \tfrac{1}{2}\sigma^2)T}{\sigma\sqrt{T}} = -0.2163,$$

$$d_2 = d_1 - \sigma\sqrt{T} = -0.2736,$$
$$N(d_1) = 0.4143, \text{ and}$$
$$N(d_2) = 0.3922.$$

Using these values to establish the value of the cash options results in

$$C = S_0 N(d_1) - Ee^{-rT}N(d_2) = \$1.59, \text{ and}$$
$$P = C - S + Ee^{-rT} = \$2.95.$$

These prices for the options on the cash security are somewhat different from those on the future because the future is not fairly priced relative to the cash security. The implied fair pricing for the future using continuous compounding is

$$F = S_0 e^{rT} = \$96.63.$$

Because the future is priced higher than its implied fair value, the futures call option is priced higher than the cash call option and the futures put option is priced lower than the cash put option.

c. Varying the value of the futures contract gives the values for the put and call options that are shown in Table E-4. Exercising the call option would be advantageous if the futures price reached a value of $109.50, because at that price, $(F - E) > C$. The put option would be exercised if the futures reached a value of $87.50, because at that price, $(E - F) > P$.

Table E-4 Values for Put and Call Options

Action	Futures Price	$(F - E)$	Call Price	Put Price
Early exercise of the call option →	$109.50	$11.50	$11.48	$ 0.06
	106.50	8.50	8.64	0.19
	103.50	5.50	5.99	0.52
	100.50	2.50	3.71	1.23
	97.50	0.50	1.98	2.48
	91.50	6.50	0.31	6.76
	89.50	8.50	0.13	8.57
Early exercise of the put option →	87.50	10.50	0.05	10.48
	85.50	12.50	0.02	12.43

Exercise 25: What is the implied volatility of a call option using the Black-Scholes model with the following parameters?

$E = \$105,$
$S_0 = \$100,$
$T = 45/365$ year,
$r = 7.0$ percent/year, and
$C = \$1.30.$

Solution: Varying the volatility in the Black-Scholes model gives the following call option prices:

Volatility Assumption	Call Price
0.18	$1.02
0.19	1.14
0.20	1.26
0.21	1.38
0.22	1.50

Table E-5   Black-Scholes Model Put and Call Options

Option	Delta	Gamma	Theta	Rho	Vega
Call Options					
E = 95	0.82	0.04	−0.04	0.06	0.08
E = 100	0.54	0.06	−0.05	0.04	0.12
E = 105	0.25	0.05	−0.04	0.02	0.09
Put Options					
E = 95	−0.18	0.04	−0.03	−0.02	0.08
E = 100	−0.46	0.06	−0.04	−0.04	0.12
E = 105	−0.75	0.05	−0.02	−0.07	0.09

Table E-6   Measures for Various Options

	Delta	Gamma	Theta	Rho	Vega
Strangle	0.36	0.10	−0.08	0.02	0.20
Short strangle	0.21	−0.11	0.08	0.02	−0.21
Strap	0.62	0.18	−0.14	0.04	0.36
Ratio spread	−0.26	−0.08	0.06	−0.02	−0.16
Covered call	0.75	−0.05	0.04	−0.02	−0.09
Protective put	0.25	0.05	−0.02	−0.07	0.09

At the current call price of $1.30, the implied volatility would be between 20 and 21 percent.

Option Sensitivities and Hedging

Exercise 26: Suppose an investor wanted to hedge a position in the underlying stock with a put option.

a. If the delta of the put option is −0.38, what position in the put option would give a delta-neutral hedge?

b. If the desired delta for the hedged position were 0.25 instead of delta-neutral, what would be the required put position?

c. What position using call options with the same strike price and maturity would give the equivalent delta to that in the question above?

Solutions:

a. The general hedge ratio between two investments is given as

$$h = \frac{\Delta_V - \Delta_1}{\Delta_2}.$$

To create a delta-neutral hedge for a security using a put option would require

$$h = \frac{0 - 1.0}{-0.38} = 2.6.$$

Consequently, 2.6 put options would have to be purchased for each security to create a delta-neutral hedge.

b. To create a positive delta of 0.25, the hedge ratio would be

$$h = \frac{0.25 - 1.0}{-0.38} = 2.0.$$

Purchasing only two put options gives a net positive delta of 0.25 for the position.

c. The delta of the equivalent call option is

$$\Delta_c = 1 + \Delta_p = 1 - 0.38 = 0.62.$$

To create a delta position of 0.25 would require 1.2 call options to be sold for each security held.

$$h = \frac{0.25 - 1.0}{0.62} = -1.2.$$

Exercise 27: Table E-5 gives sensitivity measures for various put and call options using the Black-Scholes model at $S_0 = 100$. Using these values, calculate the net sensitivity measures for each of the following strategies:

a. Strangle—Long call $(E = 100)$, long put $(E = 95)$.
b. Short strangle—Short call $(E = 105)$, short put $(E = 100)$.
c. Strap—Long two calls $(E = 100)$, long put $(E = 100)$.
d. Ratio spread—Long call $(E = 95)$, short two calls $(E = 100)$.
e. Covered call—Long stock, short call $(E = 105)$.
f. Protective put—Long stock, long put $(E = 105)$.

Solutions: The sensitivity measure for a combination of options can be calculated by summing the respective measures of each individual position. For example, the net delta of the strangle is

$$\Delta_V = \Delta_c^{100} + \Delta_p^{95} = 0.54 - 0.18 = 0.36.$$

The combined measures shown in Table E-6 are calculated from the individual option positions.

Exercise 28: Using the data in Exercise 26, calculate the hedge positions required to construct a delta/vega-neutral position using the underlying security, the call option with $E = \$100$, and the put option with $E = \$95$.

Solution: The delta-neutral constraint requires
$$\Delta_s + h_c\Delta_c + h_p\Delta_p = 0.$$
The vega-neutral constraint requires
$$v_s + h_c v_c + h_p v_p = 0.$$
Because $\Delta_s = 1$ and $v_s = 0$, the value for h_C from the vega-neutral constraint is given by

$$h_c = \frac{-h_p v_p}{v_c}.$$

Using this value in the delta-neutral constraint and solving for h_P gives

$$h_p = \frac{-\Delta_s v_c}{\Delta_p v_c - \Delta_c v_p} = \frac{-1.0(0.12)}{-0.18(0.12) - 0.54(0.08)} = 1.85.$$

Consequently, the value for h_c is

$$h_c = \frac{-1.85(0.08)}{0.12} = -1.23.$$

These hedge ratios create the delta/vega-neutral hedge. For every security held, the investor would sell 1.23 call options and buy 1.85 put options:

Position	Hedge Ratio	$h \times \Delta$	$h \times v$
Security	1.0	1.0	0.0
Call $(E = 100)$	−1.23	−0.66	−0.15
Put $(E = 95)$	1.85	−0.34	0.15
Total		0.0	0.0

Synthetic Option Positions

Exercise 29: Using the put/call parity relationship, describe which combination of securities creates each position synthetically:

a. Call option.
b. Put option.
c. Riskless bond.
d. Covered call.
e. Protective put.

   Solutions: The put/call parity relationship is given as

$$C = S_0 + P - Ee^{-rT}.$$

Therefore:

a. The synthetic call can be created by borrowing while purchasing the security plus a put option with the same maturity and exercise price.
b. The put option can be written as

$$P = C + Ee^{-rT} - S_0,$$

   which indicates that shorting the security to purchase a call option with the rest invested in a riskless bond will mimic a put option.
c. The riskless bond can be written as

$$Ee^{-rT} = S_0 + P - C.$$

   Purchasing a security plus a put option and selling a call option creates a synthetic bond.
d. A covered call would be the equivalent of

$$S_0 - C = Ee^{-rT} - P.$$

   Selling a put option and investing in a riskless bond gives the same payoff as the covered-call strategy.
e. A protective put is equivalent to

$$S_0 + P = Ee^{-rT} + C.$$

   Purchasing a call and investing in a riskless bond gives the same payoff as the protective-put strategy.

   Exercise 30: What rule should be followed to alter the mix dynamically between stock and cash to create the following positions?

a. Stock + call option.
b. Stock − put option.
c. Straddle: Long call and long put.

   Solutions: The delta of the replicating portfolio (stock and cash) is given by the fraction of the portfolio held in stock,

$$\Delta_R = \alpha.$$

To replicate another strategy dynamically, the delta of the replicating portfolio is set equal to the delta of the strategy to be replicated.

a. The delta of the desired stock and call option position is

$$\Delta_v = 1 + \Delta_c.$$

   Equating this delta to the delta of the replicating portfolio to produce a similar price movement gives

$$\alpha = 1 + \Delta_c.$$

   Because $\Delta_c > 0$, the replicating stock-plus-cash portfolio must be leveraged to replicate the stock-plus-call option payoff.

b. The delta of the stock-minus-put option position is

$$\Delta_v = 1 - \Delta_p = 1 - (\Delta_c - 1) = 2 - \Delta_c.$$

To replicate this effect, the proportion of stock in the stock-plus-cash portfolio is

$$\alpha = 2 - \Delta_c.$$

Because $\Delta_c \leq 1$, the stock-plus-cash portfolio again may have to be leveraged to achieve the desired effect.

c. The straddle position is created by being long a call and a put at the same strike price. The delta of such a position is

$$\Delta_V = \Delta_c + \Delta_p = \Delta_c + (\Delta_c - 1) = 2\Delta_c - 1.$$

To replicate this effect, the proportion of stock in the stock-plus-cash portfolio is

$$\alpha = 2\Delta_c - 1.$$

For $\Delta_c > 0.5$, the replicating portfolio's holding in stock would be positive, and for $\Delta_c < 0.5$, a short position would be required.

Appendix A: Contract Specifications for Selected Futures and Options

Futures Contracts

Contract	Contract Size	Settlement	Exchange[a]	Delivery Months	Last Trading Day	Minimum Price Change
U.S. T-bond	$100,000	U.S. T-bond, 8% 15-yr. equivalent	CBT	Mar, Jun, Sep, Dec	Business day prior to last 7 business days in contract month	1/32 point = $31.25
U.S. T-note	$100,000	U.S. T-note, 8% 6 1/2–10-yr. equivalent	CBT	Mar, Jun, Sep, Dec	Business day prior to last 7 business days in contract month	1/32 point = $31.25
U.S. T-bill	$1,000,000	U.S. T-bill, 90-day equivalent	IMM	Mar, Jun, Sep, Dec	Business day in contract month prior to issue date of new 13-week bills	0.01 point = $25.00
Eurodollars	$1,000,000	Cash settled based on 3-month Eurodollar (LIBOR) rate	IMM	Mar, Jun, Sep, Dec	Second London business day before third Wednesday of contract month	0.01 point = $25.00
Muni-bond Index	$1,000 × Index	Cash settled	CBT	Mar, Jun, Sep, Dec	Business day prior to last 7 business days of contract month	1/32 point = $31.25
S&P 500 Index	$500 × Index	Cash settled	CME	Mar, Jun, Sep, Dec	Thursday before third Friday of contract month	0.05 point = $25.00
NYSE Index	$500 × Index	Cash settled	NYFE	Mar, Jun, Sep, Dec	Thursday before third Friday of contract month	0.05 point = $25.00
Value Line Index	$500 × Index	Cash settled	KCBT	Mar, Jun, Sep, Dec	Third Friday of contract month	0.05 point = $25.00

Appendix A. (continued)
Futures Contracts (continued)

Contract	Contract Size	Settlement	Exchange[a]	Delivery Months	Last Trading Day	Minimum Price Change
Major Market Index	$500 × Index	Cash settled	CBT	Nearest three months and next month in March cycle	Third Friday of contract month	0.05 point = $25.00
British pound	25,000 BP	Delivery of foreign currency by wire transfer two days after the last day of trading	IMM	Mar, Jun, Sep, Dec	Second business day before third Wednesday of contract month	$0.0005/BP = $12.50
Canadian dollar	100,000 CD	Delivery of foreign currency by wire transfer two days after the last day of trading	IMM	Mar, Jun, Sep, Dec	Second business day before third Wednesday of contract month	$0.0001/CD = $10.00
Deutsche mark	125,000 DM	Delivery of foreign currency by wire transfer two days after the last day of trading	IMM	Mar, Jun, Sep, Dec	Second business day before third Wednesday of contract month	$0.0001/DM = $12.50
Japanese yen	12,500,000 JY	Delivery of foreign currency by wire transfer two days after the last day of trading	IMM	Mar, Jun, Sep, Dec	Second business day before third Wednesday of contract month	$0.000001/JY = $12.50
Swiss franc	125,000 SF	Delivery of foreign currency by wire transfer two days after the last day of trading	IMM	Mar, Jun, Sep, Dec	Second business day before third Wednesday of contract month	$0.0001/SF = $12.50

Appendix A. (continued)
Futures Options

Contract	Contract Size	Exchange[a]	Delivery Months	Last Trading Day	Minimum Price Change	Type of Exercise
U.S. T-bond	$100,000	CBT	Next month and subsequent two months in March cycle	Friday at least 5 business days prior to the first business day of the delivery month	1/64 point = $15.625	American
U.S. T-Note	$100,000	CBT	Next month and subsequent two months in March cycle	Friday at least 5 business days prior to the first business day for the delivery month	1/64 point = $15.625	American
U.S. T-bill	$1,000,000	IOM	Mar, Jun, Sep, Dec	Friday at least 5 business days prior to first notice day for the futures contract	0.01 point = $25.00	American
Eurodollars	$1,000,000	IOM	Mar, Jun, Sep, Dec	Last trading day of underlying futures contract	0.01 point = $25.00	American
Muni-bond Index	$100,000	CBT	Mar, Jun, Sep, Dec	Last trading day of underlying futures contract	1/64 point = $15.625	American
S&P 500 Index	$500 × Index	IOM	Nearest 3 months	Third Friday of the contract month	0.05 point = $25.00	American
NYSE Index	$500 × Index	NYFE	Nearest 3 months and subsequent month in March cycle	Thursday before third Friday of the contract month	0.05 point = $25.00	American
British pound	25,000 BP	IOM	Next 4 months plus the following 2 quarterly expirations	Second Friday prior to the third Wednesday of the expiration month	$0.0005/BP = $12.50	American
Canadian dollar	100,000 CD	IOM	Next 4 months plus the following 2 quarterly expirations	Second Friday prior to the third Wednesday of the expiration month	$0.0001/CD = $10.00	American
Deutsche mark	125,000 DM	IOM	Next 4 months plus the following 2 quarterly expirations	Second Friday prior to the third Wednesday of the expiration month	$0.0001/DM = $12.50	American
Japanese yen	12,500,000 JY	IOM	Next 4 months plus the following 2 quarterly expirations	Second Friday prior to the third Wednesday of the expiration month	$0.0000001/JY = $12.50	American
Swiss franc	125,000 SF	IOM	Next 4 months plus the following 2 quarterly expirations	Second Friday prior to the third Wednesday of the expiration month	$0.0001/SF = $12.50	American

Appendix A. (continued)
Index Options

Contract	Contract Size	Exchange[a]	Delivery Months	Last Trading Day	Minimum Price Change	Type of Exercise
S&P 100 Index (OEX)	$100 × Index	CBOE	Nearest 4 months	Third Friday of contract month	1/8 point = $12.50 for option prices greater than $3 1/16 point = $6.25 for option prices less than $3	American
S&P 500 Index (SPX)	$100 × Index	CBOE	Nearest 3 months plus the next month in March cycle	Third Friday of contract month		European
S&P 500 Index (NSX)	$100 × Index	CBOE	Mar, Jun, Sep, Dec	Third Friday of contract month (at the open)		European
Major Market Index (XMI)	$100 × Index	AMX	Nearest 3 months	Third Friday of contract month		American
Value Line Index	$100 × Index	PHX	Nearest 3 months	Third Friday of contract month		European
NYSE Index	$100 × Index	NYSE	Nearest 3 months	Third Friday of contract month		American

[a]AMX = American Stock Exchange.
CBOE = Chicago Board Options Exchange.
CBT = Chicago Board of Trade.
CME = Chicago Mercantile Exchange.
IMM = International Monetary Market at the CME.
IOM = International Options Market at the CME.
KCBT = Kansas City Board of Trade.
NYFE = New York Futures Exchange.
NYSE = New York Stock Exchange.
PHX = Philadelphia Stock Exchange.

Appendix B: Interest Rate Concepts

Interest Rate Quotations

Investors generally like to think in terms of annualized interest rates, but annualized rates can be quoted several different ways depending on the assumed compounding period. This section describes some of the common ways interest rates are quoted relative to financial securities. The particular applications discussed are for simple interest or money-market yield (for Eurodeposits and certificates of deposit), discount rate basis (for Treasury bills), a bond-equivalent yield or yield to maturity (for bonds and notes), and a continuously compounded rate of return (for theoretical models). These rates can be compared with each other by converting them to an effective annual rate.

A simple interest or money-market yield in annualized terms is equal to the amount of interest paid for t days divided by the principal multiplied by the number of periods of length t in a 360-day year. Thus, the simple interest rate is

$$r = \frac{\$ \text{ Interest}}{\text{Principal}} \left(\frac{360}{t} \right).$$

The amount of principal and interest at the end of t days is equal to

$$\text{Principal} + \text{Interest} = \text{Principal} \left(1 + \frac{rt}{360} \right).$$

In contrast to a simple interest quotation, Treasury bills are quoted on a bank discount rate basis. The discount rate represents the annualized discount taken when a Treasury bill that matures in t days is first purchased. The discount rate is calculated as the dollar discount divided by the face value of the Treasury bill multiplied by the number of periods of length t in a 360-day year:

$$d = \frac{\$ \text{ Discount}}{\text{Face value}} \left(\frac{360}{t} \right).$$

To convert from a simple interest to a bank discount rate is relatively easy. They are related by the following expression:

$$\left(1 + \frac{rt}{360}\right) = \frac{1}{1 - \dfrac{dt}{360}} \ ,$$

which gives the relationship between d and r as

$$d = \frac{r}{1 + \dfrac{rt}{360}} \ , \quad \text{and}$$

$$r = \frac{d}{1 - \dfrac{dt}{360}} \ .$$

If interest earned at annual rate y is compounded semiannually, the amount of principal and interest at the end of a year is equal to

$$\text{Principal} + \text{Interest} = \text{Principal} \left(1 + \frac{y}{2}\right)^2 .$$

The annual rate y is often called the *bond-equivalent yield* or *yield to maturity* when referring to bonds or notes that pay interest semiannually.

If interest is compounded continuously at a rate c for T portion of a year, the amount of principal and interest is equal to

$$\text{Principal} + \text{Interest} = \text{Principal} \ (e^{cT}),$$

where e is the natural exponent.

These annualized rates can be different from each other and yet all result in the same amount of principal and interest at the end of a year because of the differences in compounding assumptions or quotation conventions. The relationships among them can be seen if each is equated to the same effective annual rate, represented by i. For each $1 of principal invested at the beginning of the year, $1 + i$ represents the total of principal plus interest at the end of the year. Equating the total of principal plus interest from each type of interest quotation results in the following conventions to represent the interrelationships:

$$1 + i = \left(1 + \frac{rt}{360}\right)^{\frac{365}{t}} \quad \text{Money-market yield}$$

$$= \left(1 - \frac{dt}{360}\right)^{\frac{-365}{t}} \quad \text{Bank discount rate}$$

$$= \left(1 + \frac{y}{2}\right)^2 \quad \text{Bond-equivalent yield}$$

$$= e^{cT} \quad \text{Continuously compounded rate (annualized } T = 1)$$

To understand the relationship between these rates, consider a money-market investment that pays an annual rate of 9.30 percent for 91 days. What are the equivalent annual rates expressed using different compounding assumptions or conventions? The effective annual rate is

$$i = \left(1 + \frac{rt}{360}\right)^{\frac{365}{t}} - 1 = \left[1 + 0.093 \left(\frac{91}{360}\right)\right]^{\frac{365}{91}} - 1 = 9.77 \text{ percent.}$$

The bond-equivalent yield that gives the same effective annual rate is

$$y = 2[(1 + i)^{1/2} - 1] = 2[(1.0977)^{1/2} - 1] = 9.54 \text{ percent.}$$

The continuously compounded rate is

$$c = \frac{\ln(1 + i)}{T} = \frac{\ln(1.0977)}{1} = 9.32 \text{ percent.}$$

The equivalent rate quoted as a bank discount rate is

$$d = \frac{r}{\left(1 + \dfrac{rt}{360}\right)} = \frac{0.093}{1 + 0.093 \left(\dfrac{91}{360}\right)} = 9.09 \text{ percent.}$$

All these annualized rates are simply quoted using different compounding assumptions or conventions; they give the same effective annual rate.

Term Structure of Interest Rates and Forward Rates

The term structure describes the annualized interest rates offered in the market for various maturities. A flat term structure offers the same annual rate for a 1-year investment as for a 10-year investment. The term structure is often upward sloping: Higher rates are offered for longer maturities. Occasionally, however, the term structure is downward sloping or humped in some regions of the maturity structure.

Figure B-1 gives an example of the term structure of interest rates; i_y represents the current annual interest rate with a maturity of y years. A relationship between two different points along the term-structure curve is represented by the implied forward rate. In general, the relationship is

$$(1 + i_y)^y = (1 + i_x)^x \, (1 + {}_x f_y)^{y-x},$$

where ${}_x f_y$ is the implied annualized forward interest rate from maturity x to maturity y in years.

The forward interest rate ${}_x f_y$ represents the annualized return implied in the current term structure that an investor would receive by investing from maturity year x to year y. The rate i_x represents the rate offered for investing for x years, while i_y represents the rate offered for investing for y years. The above relationship indicates that, if an investor earns rate i_x for x years and ${}_x f_y$ between years x and y, the total return offered will be an annualized rate of i_y for y years.

Implied forward rates are important because they correspond closely with rates implied in the pricing of financial futures and forward contracts. Because current interest rates are known, implied forward rates can be calculated using the basic relationship given above.

For example, if the current two-year interest rate is i_2 and the one-year interest rate is i_1, the relationship between them and the one-year interest rate one year forward is

$$(1 + i_2)^2 = (1 + i_1) \, (1 + {}_1 f_2). \tag{B.1}$$

The rate ${}_1 f_2$ would represent the implied one-year rate (between Year 1 and Year 2) starting at Year 1 (or one year forward in time). Using the three-year interest rate, the two-year rate one year forward in time (${}_1 f_3$) can be developed:

101

$$(1 + i_3)^3 = (1 + i_1)(1 + {}_1f_3)^2. \tag{B.2}$$

One could also write the relationship as

$$(1 + i_3)^3 = (1 + i_2)^2(1 + {}_2f_3), \tag{B.3}$$

which gives the one-year rate two years forward in time. Finally, substituting Equation B.1 into B.3 gives

$$(1 + i_3)^3 = (1 + i_2)(1 + {}_1f_2)(1 + {}_2f_3),$$

which indicates that the current three-year rate can be thought of as the one-year rate times the sequence of one-year forward rates out to Year 3.

Figure B-1 also shows the term structure implied by the forward rates one year forward in time. From the current term structure of interest rates, other term structures for dates into the future can be implied.

To illustrate this process, consider the following current interest rates:

Maturity (Years)	Interest Rate (%)
1	6.4
2	6.7
3	6.8
4	7.0
5	7.3

With these five points, a partial term structure for one, two, three, and four years forward can be calculated, as illustrated in Figure B-2 and Table B-1.

For example, the one-year rate one year forward in time implied by the relationship in Equation B.1 is

$${}_1f_2 = \frac{(1 + i_2)^2}{(1 + i_1)} - 1 = \frac{(1.067)^2}{(1.064)} - 1 = 7.0 \text{ percent.}$$

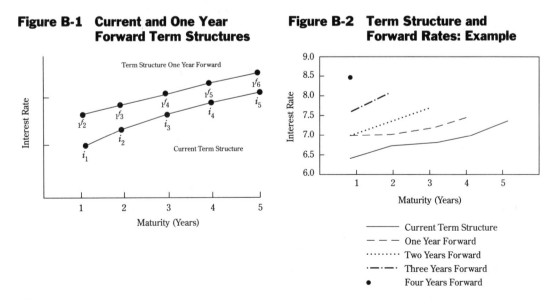

Figure B-1 Current and One Year Forward Term Structures

Figure B-2 Term Structure and Forward Rates: Example

——— Current Term Structure
— — — One Year Forward
············ Two Years Forward
·—·—· Three Years Forward
● Four Years Forward

Table B-1   Term Structure and Forward Rates: Example

Years Forward	Maturity in Years				
	1	2	3	4	5
0	6.4	6.7	6.8	7.0	7.3
1	7.0	7.0	7.2	7.5	
2	7.0	7.3	7.7		
3	7.6	8.1			
4	8.5				

The two-year rate one year forward in time comes from using Equation B.2, giving

$$_1f_3 = \left[\frac{(1 + i_3)^3}{(1 + i_1)}\right]^{1/2} - 1 = \left[\frac{(1.068)^3}{(1.064)}\right]^{1/2} - 1 = 7.0 \text{ percent.}$$

The one-year rate two years forward in time comes from using Equation B.3:

$$_2f_3 = \frac{(1 + i_3)^3}{(1 + i_1)(1 + {_1f_2})} - 1 = \frac{(1.068)^3}{(1.064)(1.07)} - 1 = 7.0 \text{ percent.}$$

Each rate can be developed in turn until the full set of forward rates implied by the current term structure is calculated.

Appendix C: Price Behavior of Fixed-Income Securities

The price of long-maturity fixed-income securities will change as interest rates change, and being able to describe how the price changes is important for those trying to hedge the price movement using derivative securities. *Duration* and *convexity* are two measures that help describe how the price of a fixed-income security changes as its yield to maturity changes.

Duration and Convexity

Suppose P represents the price of a fixed-income security and y represents its annualized yield to maturity. The change in the price of the security can be approximated using a Taylor series expansion:

$$\Delta P = \frac{dP}{dy}\,\Delta y + \tfrac{1}{2}\frac{d^2P}{dy^2}\,(\Delta y)^2 = P[-D^*\Delta y + \tfrac{1}{2}\,C^*(\Delta y)^2],$$

where

$$D^* = -\frac{1}{P}\left(\frac{dP}{dy}\right)$$

and

$$C^* = \frac{1}{P}\left(\frac{d^2P}{dy^2}\right).$$

The term D^* is usually referred to as the *modified duration*, and C^* is the (modified) *convexity*. A first-order approximation often ignores the convexity term and represents the price change simply as

$$\Delta P = -PD^*\Delta y.$$

Figure C-1 shows how the price of a security changes with respect to its yield to maturity. Duration is related to the slope of the price curve at a particular point because it is proportional to the change in the price as its yield to maturity changes. Notice that

Figure C-1   Price Behavior of Fixed-Income Securities

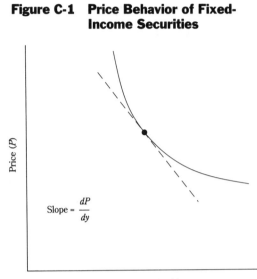

Yield to Maturity (*y*)

the price line itself has some curvature, so the slope is a less accurate approximation as the change in yield becomes greater. Convexity, a second-order term, attempts to adjust the slope approximation for this curvature.

Duration can be calculated by noting that the price of a security is equal to the present value of its interest and principal payments discounted by its yield to maturity:

$$P = \sum_{t=1}^{T} \frac{CF_t}{\left(1 + \dfrac{y}{2}\right)^t},$$ (C.1)

where T represents the total number of semiannual periods until maturity of the security, and CF_t represents the interest or principal payments in period t.

The summation process in Equation C.1 is sometimes cumbersome to handle, so an equivalent mathematical expression that eliminates the summation sign can be substituted to calculate the price of the security:

$$P = \frac{B\left(c\left[\left(1 + \dfrac{y}{2}\right)^T - 1\right] + y\right)}{y\left(1 + \dfrac{y}{2}\right)^T},$$ (C.2)

where B represents the face value of the security paid at maturity, and c represents the coupon rate on the security.

The expressions from Equations C.1 and C.2 can be used to find an expression for the modified duration of the security, or the change in the security price as the yield to maturity changes. From Equation C.1 using the summation form:

$$D^* = -\frac{1}{P}\left(\frac{dP}{dy}\right) = \frac{-1}{2\left(1 + \dfrac{y}{2}\right)} \sum_{t=1}^{T} \frac{tCF_t}{P\left(1 + \dfrac{y}{2}\right)^t},$$ (C.3)

and from Equation C.2:

$$D^* = \frac{B\left(c\left[1 + \frac{y}{2}\right]\left[\left(1 + \frac{y}{2}\right)^T - 1\right] + \frac{yT}{2}[y - c]\right)}{Py^2\left(1 + \frac{y}{2}\right)^{T+1}}.$$ (C.4)

Equation C.3 gives some additional insight into the concept of duration. The expression indicates that duration is a weighted average of the maturities of each of the cash payments, where the weights represent the proportion each discounted payment is of the initial security price. To avoid the cumbersome summation notation, Equation C.4 gives an algebraic expression for the modified duration expressed in years.

The expressions from Equations C.3 and C.4 can be used to find an expression for the modified convexity by finding the change in the slope of the price curve as the yield to maturity changes. From Equation C.3 using the summation form:

$$C^* = \frac{1}{P}\left(\frac{d^2P}{dy^2}\right) = \frac{1}{4}\frac{1}{P}\sum_{t=1}^{T}\frac{t(t + 1)CF_t}{\left(1 + \frac{y}{2}\right)^{t+2}},$$ (C.5)

and from Equation C.4:

$$C^* = \frac{B\left(2c\left[1 + \frac{y}{2}\right]^2\left[\left(1 + \frac{y}{2}\right)^T - 1\right] - cyT\left[1 + \frac{y}{2}\right] + y^2T[T + 1]\frac{[y - c]}{4}\right)}{Py^3\left(1 + \frac{y}{2}\right)^{T+2}}.$$ (C.6)

To illustrate the use of duration and convexity, consider the case of a bond with a coupon rate of 8 percent paid semiannually and a yield to maturity of 9 percent. The face value of the bond is $1,000 with six years to maturity. The value of the bond, using Equation C.2, is

$$P = \frac{B\left(\left[c\left[\left(1 + \frac{y}{2}\right)^T - 1\right] + y\right]\right)}{y\left(1 + \frac{y}{2}\right)^T} = 1000\frac{(0.08[(1.045)^{12} - 1] + 0.09)}{0.09(1.045)^{12}} = \$954.41.$$

The modified duration, using Equation C.4 is

$$D^* = \frac{B\left(c\left[1 + \frac{y}{2}\right]\left[\left(1 + \frac{y}{2}\right)^T - 1\right] + \left[\frac{yT}{2}\right][y - c]\right)}{Py^2\left(1 + \frac{y}{2}\right)^{T+1}}$$

$$= 1000\frac{\left(0.08[1.045][(1.045)^{12} - 1] + \frac{0.09(12)}{2}[0.09 - 0.08]\right)}{954.41(0.09)^2(1.045)^{13}} = 4.64 \text{ years}.$$

The convexity, using Equation C.6, is

$$C^* = B\frac{\left(2c\left[1 + \frac{y}{2}\right]^2\left[\left(1 + \frac{y}{2}\right)^T - 1\right] - cyT\left[1 + \frac{y}{2}\right] + y^2T[T + 1]\frac{[y-c]}{4}\right)}{Py^3\left(1 + \frac{y}{2}\right)^{T+2}}$$

$$= \frac{1000\left(2[0.08][1.045]^2[(1.045)^{12} - 1] - 0.08[0.09][12][1.045] + [0.09]^2[12][13]\frac{[0.09 - 0.08]}{4}\right)}{954.41(0.09)^3(1.045)^{14}}$$

$$= 26.74.$$

From the duration and convexity measures, the price change from a 0.2 percent increase in yield to maturity can be approximated by using the Taylor series expansion:

$$\Delta P = P[-D^*\Delta y + 1/2C^*(\Delta y)^2] = 954.41[-4.64(0.002) + 1/2(26.74)(0.002)^2]$$

$$= -\$8.81.$$

The actual price of the security, using Equation C.2, which now has a 9.2 percent yield to maturity after the change in interest rates, is

$$P = \$945.60,$$

giving an actual price change of

$$\Delta P = (945.60 - 954.41) = -\$8.81.$$

The approximation, using the duration and convexity measures for a small change in yield to maturity, is –$8.81, which rounded to two decimal places is equal to the actual price change, –$8.81.

Implied Duration of a Bond or Note Futures Contract

Although a futures contract is not usually thought of as having a series of cash flows over time like a fixed-income security, the duration of a futures contract can be implied from its relationship to the underlying cheapest-to-deliver (CTD) note or bond. The fair value of the futures contract is given as

$$F = \frac{P\left(1 + \frac{rt}{360}\right) - Bc\frac{(t + a)}{365}}{f},$$

where

P = price of the CTD note or bond + accrued interest,

t = days to maturity of the futures contract,

r = annualized interest rate to maturity t,

a = days of accrued interest,

c = annualized coupon rate of the CTD note or bond,

B = face value of the CTD note or bond, and

f = delivery factor of the CTD note or bond.

Taking the derivative of F with respect to the yield to maturity of the CTD security gives the implied futures duration as

$$D_F^* = -\frac{1}{F}\left(\frac{dF}{dy}\right) = \frac{P}{fF}\left[D^*\left(1 + \frac{rt}{360}\right) - \left(\frac{dr}{dy}\right)\frac{t}{360}\right], \tag{C.7}$$

where D^* is the modified duration of the CTD security. The term dr/dy represents the change in the short-term interest rate as the yield to maturity changes. The duration of the futures contract is important to know for the same reason that the duration of the underlying security is important: To hedge the price movement of the underlying security as interest rates change, one must know how the security price changes and how the futures price changes. The durations of the security and the futures contract help describe the relative price sensitivities to changes in interest rates.

For example, consider a bond plus accrued interest priced at $103^{10}/_{32}$ with a modified duration of 10.1 years and a delivery factor of 1.1106. The future is priced at $99^{16}/_{32}$ with a maturity of 65 days. If the short-term interest rate is 7.3 percent and short-term rates are expected to move parallel to long-term rates, the duration of the futures contract, using Equation C.7, is

$$D_F^* = \frac{103.31}{1.1106(99.50)}\left[10.1\left(1 + 0.073\frac{65}{360}\right)\right) - (1.0)\left(\frac{65}{360}\right)\right] = 9.4 \text{ years.}$$

The delivery factors for each eligible bond or note are calculated for each futures expiration date under the assumption that the security has a standardized 8 percent yield to maturity. The ratio of the price of the individual bond to that of an 8 percent coupon bond with both having an 8 percent yield to maturity represents the delivery factor. For example, the price of a 9 percent coupon bond with an 8 percent yield to maturity due in five years, using Equation C.2, is

$$P = \frac{100[0.09(1.04^{10} - 1) + 0.08]}{0.08(1.04)^{10}} = \$104.06.$$

The delivery factor when the security has five years before maturity is

$$f = \frac{P}{100} = 1.0406.$$

The factor associated with a bond having a coupon rate greater than 8 percent always exceeds 1. Conversely, the factor associated with a bond having a coupon rate less than 8 percent is always less than 1.

The investor with the short futures position has the choice of which security to deliver against the futures position. The short seller receives at delivery the futures price times the delivery factor plus accrued interest. The security to be delivered would cost the investor the purchase price (P) plus accrued interest. The CTD security would be the security with the minimum net cost:

$$CTD = \text{Security with minimum value of } (P - F \times f)$$

$$= \text{Security with minimum value of } P/f.$$

The second equality follows because given a fixed futures price F, minimizing the minimum net cost is equivalent to minimizing the factor-adjusted security price.

Which bond is cheapest to deliver depends on duration and yield. Suppose bonds are trading at the same yield to maturity. If the yield to maturity is below 8 percent, then the bond with the shortest duration is generally the cheapest to deliver. If the yield to

Table C-1 Cheapest-to-Deliver Bond at Expiration

Maturity in Years	Coupon Rate	Yield to Maturity	Modified Duration	Bond Price (P)	Delivery Factor (f)	P/f
20	9.0	8.0	9.7	109.89	1.0989	100.00
20	7.0	8.0	10.2	90.10	.9010	100.00
20	7.0	7.0	10.7	100.00	.9010	110.99
20	9.0	7.0	10.2	121.36	1.0989	110.44
20	7.0	9.0	9.7	81.60	.9010	90.57[a]
20	9.0	9.0	9.2	100.00	1.0989	91.00

[a]Cheapest to deliver.

maturity is above 8 percent, then the bond with the longest duration is generally cheapest to deliver. Among bonds having the same duration, the bond with the highest yield to maturity is generally the cheapest to deliver. Notice that these general relationships hold in Table C-1, which illustrates the CTD security.

As yields change, the CTD security changes, and this change causes the futures contract to follow a different security than it did previously, which may change the duration of the futures contract. Figure C-2 illustrates the shift in cheapest to deliver for the 1990 Treasury-bond futures contract and the resulting jumps in the duration of the futures contract as interest rates change. The investor must make adjustments in the parameters of the hedge to accommodate this occasional shift in duration. For example, as long as the yield on the Treasury bond due in 2016 with a coupon of 7.5 percent stays above 9 percent, that same bond was the cheapest to deliver against the 1990 bond contract. As interest rates fall below 9 percent, the cheapest to deliver switches to the Treasury bond due in 2012 with a coupon of 10⅜ percent. Notice that the duration of the futures contract suddenly drops from more than 10.5 years to less than 9.5 years.

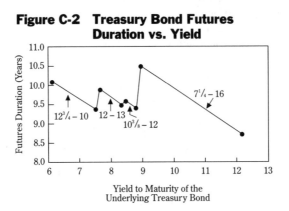

Figure C-2 Treasury Bond Futures Duration vs. Yield

Note: The notation 7¼–16 refers to the Treasury bond due in 2016 with a coupon of 7.25 percent.

Appendix D: Cumulative Normal Distribution

Standard Normal Probabilities

The standard normal distribution table, Table D-1, can be used to assess the probability that an observed value will be greater than or equal to or less than or equal to a given value. Suppose an analyst wants to know the probability of observing a value equal to or greater than -1.42. Looking in the 1.4 row/0.02 column of the table gives the value 0.9222, which is the probability of observing a value less than or equal to -1.42. Subtract this number from 1. The answer is 0.0778; that is, there is a 7.78 percent likelihood that the observed value will be greater than or equal to -1.42.

Because the table is symmetric, negative values need not be shown separately. The probability of observing a value x less than or equal to -1.42 is the same as that of observing a value x greater than or equal to 1.42, $\text{Prob}(x \leq d) = \text{Prob}(x \geq -d)$. The probability of observing a value x greater than or equal to 1.42 is 1 minus the probability of observing a value x less than or equal to 1.42, $\text{Prob}(x \geq -d) = 1 - \text{Prob}(x \leq -d)$.

Numerical Algorithm for the Cumulative Normal Distribution

Sometimes using an algorithm to calculate the cumulative normal distribution is more useful than using the precalculated table. The following algorithm can be used to calculate the cumulative normal distribution and is accurate to 0.0002:

$$N(d) = 1 - (a_1 k + a_2 k^2 + a_3 k^3) n(d) \text{ when } d \geq 0$$

$$N(d) = 1 - N(-d) \text{ when } d < 0,$$

where $k = \dfrac{1}{1 + ad}$, $a = 0.33267$, $a_1 = 0.4361836$, $a_2 = -0.1201676$, $a_3 = 0.9372980$, and $n(d) = 1/\sqrt{2\pi}\ e^{-d^2/2}$.

Table D-1   Standard Normal Distribution

d	0.00	0.01	0.02	0.03	Prob $(x \le d) = N(d)$ 0.04	0.05	0.06	0.07	0.08	0.09
0.0	.5000	.5040	.5080	.5120	.5160	.5199	.5239	.5279	.5319	.5359
0.1	.5398	.5438	.5478	.5517	.5557	.5596	.5636	.5675	.5714	.5753
0.2	.5793	.5832	.5871	.5910	.5948	.5987	.6026	.6064	.6103	.6141
0.3	.6179	.6217	.6255	.6293	.6331	.6368	.6406	.6443	.6480	.6517
0.4	.6554	.6591	.6628	.6664	.6700	.6736	.6772	.6808	.6844	.6879
0.5	.6915	.6950	.6985	.7019	.7054	.7088	.7123	.7157	.7190	.7224
0.6	.7257	.7291	.7324	.7357	.7389	.7422	.7454	.7486	.7517	.7549
0.7	.7580	.7611	.7642	.7673	.7704	.7734	.7764	.7794	.7823	.7852
0.8	.7881	.7910	.7939	.7967	.7995	.8023	.8051	.8078	.8106	.8133
0.9	.8159	.8186	.8212	.8238	.8264	.8289	.8315	.8340	.8365	.8389
1.0	.8413	.8438	.8461	.8485	.8508	.8531	.8554	.8577	.8599	.8621
1.1	.8643	.8665	.8686	.8708	.8729	.8749	.8770	.8790	.8810	.8830
1.2	.8849	.8860	.8888	.8907	.8925	.8943	.8962	.8980	.8997	.9015
1.3	.9032	.9049	.9066	.9082	.9099	.9115	.9131	.9147	.9162	.9177
1.4	.9192	.9207	.9222	.9236	.9251	.9265	.9279	.9292	.9306	.9319
1.5	.9332	.9345	.9357	.9370	.9382	.9394	.9406	.9418	.9429	.9441
1.6	.9452	.9463	.9474	.9484	.9495	.9505	.9515	.9525	.9535	.9545
1.7	.9554	.9564	.9573	.9582	.9591	.9599	.9688	.9616	.9625	.9633
1.8	.9641	.9649	.9656	.9664	.9671	.9678	.9686	.9693	.9699	.9706
1.9	.9713	.9719	.9726	.9732	.9738	.9744	.9750	.9756	.9761	.9767
2.0	.9772	.9778	.9783	.9788	.9793	.9798	.9803	.9808	.9812	.9817
2.1	.9821	.9826	.9830	.9834	.9838	.9842	.9846	.9850	.9854	.9857
2.2	.9861	.9864	.9868	.9871	.9875	.9878	.9881	.9884	.9887	.9890
2.3	.9893	.9896	.9898	.9901	.9904	.9906	.9909	.9911	.9913	.9916
2.4	.9918	.9920	.9922	.9925	.9927	.9929	.9931	.9932	.9934	.9936
2.5	.9938	.9940	.9941	.9943	.9945	.9946	.9948	.9949	.9951	.9952
2.6	.9953	.9955	.9956	.9957	.9959	.9960	.9961	.9962	.9963	.9964
2.7	.9965	.9966	.9967	.9968	.9969	.9970	.9971	.9972	.9973	.9974
2.8	.9974	.9975	.9976	.9977	.9977	.9978	.9979	.9979	.9980	.9981
2.9	.9981	.9982	.9982	.9983	.9984	.9984	.9985	.9985	.9986	.9986
3.0	.9987	.9987	.9987	.9988	.9988	.9989	.9989	.9989	.9990	.9990

References

General References on Futures

Arak, Marcelle, Laurie Goodman, and Susan Ross. 1986. "The Cheapest to Deliver Bond on Treasury Bond Futures Contract." In *Advances in Futures and Options Research*, 1, Part B, edited by Frank Fabozzi, 49–74. Greenwich, CT: JAI Press.

Black, Fischer. 1976. "The Pricing of Commodity Contracts." *Journal of Financial Economics* (January/February):167–79.

Bookstaber, Richard M. 1985. *The Complete Investment Book*. Glenview, Ill.: Scott, Foresman.

Chance, D. 1989. *An Introduction to Options and Futures*. Chicago: The Dryden Press.

Hull, J. 1989. *Options, Futures, and Other Derivative Securities*. Englewood Cliffs, N.J.: Prentice-Hall.

Johnson, L.L. 1960. "The Theory of Hedging and Speculation in Commodity Futures Markets." *Review of Economic Studies* (October):139–51.

Kolb, Robert W. 1985. *Understanding Futures Markets*. Glenview, Ill.: Scott, Foresman.

———. 1982. *Interest Rate Futures: A Comprehensive Introduction*. Richmond, Va.: R. F. Dame.

Kolb, Robert W., and Gerald D. Gay, eds. 1982. *Interest Rate Futures: Concepts and Issues*. Richmond, Va.: R. F. Dame.

Kolb, Robert W., Gerald D. Gay, and William C. Hunter. 1985. "Liquidity Requirements for Financial Futures Hedges." *Financial Analysts Journal* (May/June):60–68.

Powers, Mark J. 1984. *Inside the Financial Futures Markets*, 2nd ed. New York: John Wiley & Sons.

Schwarz, Edward W., Joanne M. Hill, and Thomas Schneeweis. 1986. *Financial Futures: Fundamentals, Strategies, and Applications*. Homewood, Ill.: Business One Irwin.

Sharpe, William F. 1985. *Investments*, 3rd ed. Englewood Cliffs, N.J.: Prentice-Hall.

Siegel, Daniel R., and Diane F. Siegel. 1990. *Futures Markets*. Chicago: The Dryden Press.

General References on Hedging

Ahmadi, Hamid Z., Peter A. Sharp, and Carl H. Walther. 1986. "The Effectiveness of Futures and Options in Hedging Currency Risk." In *Advances in Futures and Options Research*, 1, Part B, edited by Frank Fabozzi, 171–91. Greenwich, CT: JAI Press.

Ederington, Louis H. 1979. "The Hedging Performance of the New Futures Market." *Journal of Finance* (March):157–70.

Figlewski, Stephen. 1986. *Hedging with Financial Futures for Institutional Investors*, Chapter 1. Cambridge, Mass: Ballinger Publishing Company.

———. 1984. "Hedging Performance and Basis Risk in Stock Index Futures." *Journal of Finance* (July):657–69.

Gay, Gerald D., Robert W. Kolb, and Raymond Chiang. 1983. "Interest Rate Hedging: An Empirical Test of Alternative Strategies." *Journal of Financial Research* (Fall):187–97.

Hill, Joanne, and Thomas Schneeweis. 1982. "The Hedging Effectiveness of Foreign Currency Futures." *Journal of Financial Research* (Spring):95–104.

Kolb, Robert W., and Raymond Chiang. 1981. "Improving Hedging Performance Using Interest Rate Futures." *Financial Management* (Autumn):72–79.

Kolb, Robert W., and Gerald D. Gay, eds. 1982. "Risk Reduction Potential of Financial Futures for Corporate Bond Positions." In *Interest Rate Futures: Concepts and Issues.* Richmond, Va.: R. F. Dame.

Empirical Research Concerning Forward and Futures Prices

Cornell, B., and M. Reinganum. 1981. "Forward and Futures Prices: Evidence from Foreign Exchange Markets." *Journal of Finance* (December):1035–45.

French, K. 1983. "A Comparison of Futures and Forward Prices." *Journal of Financial Economics* (November):311–42.

Park, H.Y., and A.H. Chen. 1985. "Differences Between Futures and Forward Prices: A Further Investigation of Marking to Market Effects." *Journal of Futures Markets* (February):77–88.

Rendleman, R., and C. Carabini. 1979. "The Efficiency of the Treasury Bill Futures Markets." *Journal of Finance* (September):895–914.

Theoretical Relationship Between Forward and Futures Prices

Cox, J.C., J.E. Ingersoll, and S.A. Ross. 1981. "The Relation Between Forward Prices and Futures Prices." *Journal of Financial Economics* (December):321–46.

Jarrow, R.A., and G.S. Oldfield. 1981. "Forward Contracts and Futures Contracts." *Journal of Financial Economics* (December):373–82.

Kane, E.J. 1980. "Market Incompleteness and Divergences Between Forward and Futures Interest Rates." *Journal of Finance* (May):221–34.

Richard, S., and M. Sundaresan. 1981. "A Continuous Time Model of Forward and Futures Prices in a Multigood Economy." *Journal of Financial Economics* (December):347–72.

General References on Options

Black, Fischer. 1975. "Fact and Fantasy in the Use of Options." *Financial Analysts Journal* (July/August):36–41, 61–72.

Black, Fischer, and Myron Scholes. 1973. "The Pricing of Options and Corporate Liabilities." *Journal of Political Economy* (May/June):637–59.

Bookstaber, Richard M. 1991. *Option Pricing and Investment Strategies.* Chicago: Probus Publishing Company.

———. 1985. *The Complete Investment Book.* Glenview, Ill.: Scott, Foresman.

Chance, D. 1989. *An Introduction to Options and Futures.* Chicago: The Dryden Press.

Choie, K., and F. Novomestky. 1989. "Replication of Long-Term with Short-Term Options." *The Journal of Portfolio Management* (Winter):17–19.

Cox, John C., and Mark Rubinstein. 1985. *Options Markets.* Englewood Cliffs, N.J.: Prentice-Hall.

Dengler, W.H., and H.P. Becker. 1984. "19 Option Strategies and When To Use Them." *Futures* (June).

Figlewski, S., W. Silber, and M. Subrahmanyam, eds. 1990. *Financial Options: From Theory to Practice.* Salomon Brothers Center for the Study of Financial Institutions. Homewood, Ill.: Business One Irwin.

Hull, J. 1989. *Options, Futures, and Other Derivative Securities.* Englewood Cliffs, N.J.: Prentice-Hall.

Jarrow, Robert, and Andrew Rudd. 1983. *Option Pricing.* Homewood, Ill.: Business One Irwin.

McMillan, Lawrence G. 1986. *Options as a Strategic Investment,* 2nd ed. New York: New York Institute of Finance.

Merton, Robert C. 1973a. "The Relationship Between Put and Call Option Prices: Comment." *Journal of Finance* (March):183–84.

———. 1973b. "The Theory of Rational Option Pricing." *Bell Journal of Economics and Management Science* (Spring):141–83.

Ritchken, Peter. 1987. *Options: Theory, Strategy, and Applications.* Glenview, Ill.: Scott, Foresman.

Sharpe, William F. 1985. *Investments,* 3rd ed. Englewood Cliffs, N.J.: Prentice-Hall.

Stoll, Hans R. 1969. "The Relationship Between Put and Call Option Prices." *Journal of Finance* (May):319–32.

Yates, James W., Jr., and Robert W. Kopprasch, Jr. 1980. "Writing Covered Call Options: Profits and Risks." *Journal of Portfolio Management* (Fall):74–80.

Black-Scholes Model and its Extensions

Black, Fischer. 1988. "How to Use the Holes in Black-Scholes." *Risk* (March).

Cox, John C., and Stephen A. Ross. 1976. "The Valuation of Options for Alternative Stochastic Processes." *Journal of Financial Economics* (March):145–60.

Cox, John C., Stephen A. Ross, and Mark Rubinstein. 1979. "Option Pricing: A Simplified Approach." *Journal of Financial Economics* (September):229–63.

Cox, John C., and Mark Rubinstein. 1983. "A Survey of Alternative Option Pricing Models." In *Option Pricing,* edited by Menachem Brenner. Lexington, Mass.: Heath.

Geske, R. 1979. "The Valuation of Compound Options." *Journal of Financial Economics* 7:63–81.

Hull, J., and A. White. 1987. "The Pricing of Options on Assets with Stochastic Volatilities." *Journal of Finance* (June):281–300.

Merton, Robert C. 1976. "Option Pricing When Underlying Stock Returns are Discontinuous." *Journal of Financial Economics* (March):125–44.

Rubinstein, M. 1983. "Displaced Diffusion Option Pricing." *Journal of Finance* (March):213–17.

Smith, Clifford W., Jr. 1976. "Option Pricing: A Review." *Journal of Financial Economics* (January/March):3–51.

Binomial Models

Boyle, P.P. 1988. "A Lattice Framework for Option Pricing with Two State Variables." *Journal of Financial and Quantitative Analysis* (March):1–12.

Cox, John C., Stephen A. Ross, and Mark Rubinstein. 1979. "Option Pricing: A Simplified Approach." *Journal of Financial Economics* (September):229–63.

Hsia, Chi-Cheng. 1983. "On Binomial Option Pricing." *Journal of Financial Research* (Spring):41–50.

Hull, J., and A. White. 1988. "The Use of the Control Variate Technique in Option Pricing." *Journal of Financial and Quantitative Analysis* (September):237–51.

Option Volatilities

Beckers, S. 1981. "Standard Deviations in Option Prices as Predictors of Future Stock Price Variability." *Journal of Banking and Finance* (September):363–82.

Bookstaber, Richard M., and Steven Pomerantz. 1989. "An Information-Based Model of Market Volatility." *Financial Analysts Journal* (November/December):37–46.

Chiras, D.P., and S. Manaster. 1978. "The Information Content of Option Prices and a Test of Market Efficiency." *Journal of Financial Economics* 6:213–34.

Whaley, Robert E. 1982. "Valuation of American Call Options on Dividend-paying Stocks: Empirical Tests." *Journal of Financial Economics* (March):29–58.

Pricing American Options and Other Approaches

Barone-Adesi, G., and R.E. Whaley. 1987. "Efficient Analytic Approximation of American Option Values." *Journal of Finance* (June):301–20.

Boyle, P.P. 1977. "Options: A Monte Carlo Approach." *Journal of Financial Economics* 4:323–38.

Brennan, M.J., and E.S. Schwartz. 1978. "Finite Difference Methods and Jump Processes Arising in the Pricing of Contingent Claims: A Synthesis." *Journal of Financial and Quantitative Analysis* (September):462–74.

———. 1977. "The Valuation of American Put Options." *Journal of Finance* (May):449–62.

Courtadon, G. 1982. "A More Accurate Finite Difference Approximation for the Valuation of Options." *Journal of Financial and Quantitative Analysis* (December):697–705.

Geske, Robert. 1981. "Comments on Whaley's Note." *Journal of Financial Economics* (June):213–15.

———. 1979. "A Note on an Analytic Formula for Unprotected American Call Options on Stocks with Known Dividends." *Journal of Financial Economics* (December):375–80.

Geske, R., and H.E. Johnson. 1984. "The American Put Valued Analytically." *Journal of Finance* (December):1511–24.

Hull, J., and A. White. 1990. "Valuing Derivative Securities Using the Explicit Finite Difference Method." *Journal of Financial and Quantitative Analysis* (March):87–100.

Johnson, H.E. 1983. "An Analytic Approximation to the American Put Price." *Journal of Financial and Quantitative Analysis* (March):141–48.

MacMillan, L.W. 1986. "Analytic Approximation for the American Put Option." In *Advances in Futures and Options Research* 1, edited by Frank Fabozzi, 119–39. Greenwich, CT: JAI Press, Inc.

Roll, Richard. 1977. "An Analytic Valuation Formula for Unprotected American Call Options on Stocks with Known Dividends." *Journal of Financial Economics* (November):251–58.

Whaley, Robert E. 1982. "Valuation of American Call Options on Dividend Paying Stocks: Empirical Tests." *Journal of Financial Economics* (March):29–58.

———. 1981. "On the Valuation of American Call Options On Stocks with Known Dividends." *Journal of Financial Economics* (June):207–12.

115

Options on Futures

Brenner, M., G. Courtadon, and M. Subrahmanyam. 1985. "Options on the Spot and Options on Futures." *Journal of Finance* (December):1303–17.

Ramaswami, K., and S.M. Sundaresan. 1985. "The Valuation of Options on Futures Contracts." *Journal of Finance* (December):1319–40.

Shastri, Kuldeep, and Kishore Tandon. 1986. "Options on Futures Contracts: A Comparison of European and American Pricing Models." *Journal of Futures Markets* (Winter):593–618.

Whaley, Robert E. 1986. "Valuation of American Futures Options: Theory and Tests." *Journal of Finance* (March):127–50.

Wolf, A. 1982. "Fundamentals of Commodity Options on Futures." *Journal of Futures Markets* 2:391–408.

Options on Currencies

Biger, Naham, and John Hull. 1983. "The Valuation of Currency Options." *Financial Management* (Spring):24–28.

Bodurtha, J.N., and G.R. Courtadon. 1987. "Tests of an American Option Pricing Model on the Foreign Currency Options Market." *Journal of Financial and Quantitative Analysis* (June):153–67.

Garman, M.B., and S.W. Kohlhagen. 1983. "Foreign Currency Option Values." *Journal of International Money and Finance* (December):231–53.

Grabbe, J.O. 1983. "The Pricing of Call and Put Options on Foreign Exchange." *Journal of International Money and Finance* (December):239–53.

Options on Bonds

Black, Fischer, Emanuel Derman, and William Toy. 1990. "A One-Factor Model of Interest Rates and Its Application to Treasury Bond Options." *Financial Analysts Journal* (January/February):33–39.

Bookstaber, R., and J. McDonald. 1985. "A Generalized Option Valuation Model for the Pricing of Bond Options." *Review of Futures Markets* 4:60–73.

Dattatreya, R., and F. Fabozzi. 1989. "A Simplified Model for Valuing Debt Options." *Journal of Portfolio Management* (Spring):64–73.

Empirical Research on Option Pricing

Black, Fischer, and Myron Scholes. 1972. "The Valuation of Option Contracts and a Test of Market Efficiency." *Journal of Finance* (May):399–418.

Bodurtha, J.N., and G.R. Courtadon. 1987. "Tests of an American Option Pricing Model on the Foreign Currency Options Market." *Journal of Financial and Quantitative Analysis* (June):153–68.

Chance, D.M. 1986. "Empirical Tests of the Pricing of Index Call Options." In *Advances in Futures and Options Research* 1, edited by Frank Fabozzi, 141–66. Greenwich, CT: JAI Press, Inc.

Chiras, D., and S. Manaster. 1978. "The Information Content of Option Prices and a Test of Market Efficiency." *Journal of Financial Economics* (September):213–34.

Galai, D. 1977. "Tests of Market Efficiency and the Chicago Board Options Exchange." *Journal of Business* (April):167–97.

Klemkosky, R.C., and B. G. Resnick. 1979. "Put-Call Parity and Market Efficiency." *Journal of Finance* (December):1141–55.

MacBeth, J.D., and L.J. Merville. 1979. "An Empirical Examination of the Black-Scholes Call Option Pricing Model." *Journal of Finance* (December):1172–86.

Shastri, K., and K. Tandon. 1986a. "An Empirical Test of a Valuation Model for American Options on Futures Contracts." *Journal of Financial and Quantitative Analysis* (December):377–92.

———. 1986b. "Valuation of Foreign Currency Options: Some Empirical Tests." *Journal of Financial and Quantitative Analysis* (June):145–60.

Performance Evaluation of Options

Bookstaber, Richard M. 1986. "The Use of Options in Performance Structuring: Modeling Returns to Meet Investment Objectives." In *Controlling Interest Rate Risk: New Techniques and Applications for Money Management*, Robert B. Platt, ed. New York: John Wiley & Sons.

Bookstaber, Richard M., and Roger Clarke. 1985. "Problems in Evaluating the Performance of Portfolios with Options." *Financial Analysts Journal* (January/February):48–62.

Brooks, Robert, Haim Levy, and Jim Yoder. 1987. "Using Stochastic Dominance to Evaluate the Performance of Portfolios with Options." *Financial Analysts Journal* (March/April):79–82.

Clarke, R. 1987. "Stochastic Dominance Properties of Option Strategies." In *Advances in Futures and Options Research* 2, edited by Frank Fabozzi, 1–18. Greenwich, CT: JAI Press, Inc.

Slivka, Ronald T. 1980. "Risk and Return for Option Investment Strategies." *Financial Analysts Journal* (September/October):67–73.

Glossary

American option. An option that can be exercised at any time during its life.

Anticipatory hedge. A long anticipatory hedge is initiated by buying futures contracts to protect against a rise in the price of an asset to be purchased at a later date. A short anticipatory hedge is initiated by selling futures contracts to protect against the decline in price of an asset to be sold at a future date.

Arbitrage. A transaction based on the observation of the same or an equivalent asset selling at two different prices. The transaction involves buying the asset at the lower price and selling it at the higher price.

At the money. An option in which the price of the underlying stock or future equals the exercise price.

Backwardation. A condition in financial markets in which the forward or futures price is less than the expected future spot price.

Bank discount rate. A rate quoted on short-term, noninterest-bearing money-market securities. The rate represents the annualized percentage discount from face value at the time the security is purchased.

Basis. Price difference between the underlying physical commodity and the futures contract. Cash price minus the futures price equals the basis. For some futures, such as stock index futures that are usually priced above the cash price, the basis is often calculated as the futures price minus the cash price so that the basis is a positive number.

Bear spread. An option or futures spread designed to profit in a bear market.

Bear put spread. An option strategy consisting of a long put and a short put at a lower strike price with the same maturity for both put options.

Beta. A measure of the responsiveness of a security or portfolio to the market as a whole. The term is generally used in the context of equity securities.

Binomial pricing model. A model based on the assumption that at any point in time, the price of the underlying asset or futures contract can change to one of only two possible values.

Black model. A pricing model developed by Fischer Black for a European option on a forward contract.

Black-Scholes model. A pricing model developed by Fischer Black and Myron Scholes for a European option on an asset or security.

Bond-equivalent yield. The annualized yield on a short-term instrument adjusted so as to be comparable to the yield to maturity on coupon-bearing securities (usually assumed to be compounded semiannually).

Box spread. An option strategy composed of a long bull call spread and a long bear put spread with identical strike prices and time to expiration for each spread.

Break-even point. The security price (or prices) at which a particular option strategy neither makes money nor loses money. It is generally calculated at the expiration date of the options involved in the strategy.

Bull spread. An option or futures spread designed to profit in a bull market.

Bull call spread. An option strategy consisting of a long call and a short call at a higher exercise price, with the same maturity for both call options.

Butterfly spread. An option transaction consisting of one long call at a particular exercise price, another otherwise identical long call at a higher exercise price, and two otherwise identical short calls at an exercise price between the other two.

Calendar spread. An option transaction consisting of the purchase of an option with a given expiration and the sale of an otherwise identical option with a different expiration. Also referred to as a horizontal spread.

Call option. An option that gives the holder the right to buy the underlying security at a specific price for a certain, fixed period of time.

Carry ("cost of carry"). A term associated with financing a commodity or cash security until it is sold or delivered. This can include storage, insurance, and assay expenses, but usually refers only to the financing costs on repos, bank loans, or dealer loans used to purchase the security or asset.

Cash-and-carry arbitrage. A theoretically riskless transaction of a long position in the spot asset and a short position in the futures contract that is designed to be held until the future expires. Such a transaction should earn the short-term riskless rate to eliminate any arbitrage profits.

Cash instrument. The underlying security for which futures or options are traded.

Cash settlement. The feature of certain futures contracts or options that allows delivery or exercise to be conducted with an exchange of cash rather than the physical transfer of assets.

Certificate of deposit (CD). A time deposit, usually with a bank or savings institution, having a specific maturity, which is evidenced by a certificate.

Cheapest to deliver. The bond or note that, if delivered on the Chicago Board of Trade's Treasury bond or note contract, provides the smallest difference between the invoice price and the cost of the bond or note.

Clearinghouse. An agency connected with a commodity exchange through which all futures contracts are reconciled, settled, guaranteed, and later either offset or fulfilled through delivery of the commodity and through which financial settlement is made. It may be a fully chartered, separate corporation rather than a division of the exchange itself.

Clearing member. Member of a commodity exchange who is also a member of the clearinghouse.

Closing transaction. A trade that reduces an investor's position. Closing buy transactions reduce short positions and closing sell transactions reduce long positions.

Collar. An option strategy consisting of a long position in an underlying security and a short call and a long put with equal expiration dates; the call has a higher strike price than the put.

Commodity Futures Trading Commission (CFTC). An independent federal regulatory agency charged and empowered under the Commodity Futures Trading Commission Act of 1974 with regulation of futures trading and all futures options in all commodities. The CFTC's responsibilities include examining and approving all contracts before they may be traded on the exchange floor.

Commodity pool. An investment arrangement in which individuals combine their funds and the total amount of funds is used to trade futures contracts, with a large cash reserve set aside to meet margin calls.

Commodity trading advisor. An individual who specializes in offering advice regarding the trading of futures contracts.

Condor. An option position consisting of two otherwise identical short call positions at separate strike prices and two long call positions at strike prices outside the strike prices of the two short positions.

Contango. A condition in financial markets in which the forward or futures price is greater than the expected future spot price.

Continuously compounded return. A rate of return between two points in time in which the asset price is assumed to grow or pay a return at a continuous rate.

Convergence. The narrowing of the basis as a futures contract approaches expiration.

Conversion factor. An adjustment factor applied to the settlement price of the Chicago Board of Trade's Treasury bond and note contracts that gives the holder of the short position a choice of several different bonds or notes to deliver.

Convexity. A measure of the curvature of a bond's price line as interest rates change. It is often used along with duration to approximate the change in the price of a bond as its yield to maturity changes.

Coupon rate. The rate of interest stated on a bond to be paid to the purchaser by the issuer of the bond. Interest payments on a bond are generally paid semiannually and are equal to the coupon rate times the face value prorated for the payment period.

Covered call. A combination of a long position in an asset, futures contract, or currency and a short position in a call on the same.

Covered interest arbitrage. The purchasing of an instrument denominated in a foreign currency and hedging the resulting foreign exchange risk by selling the proceeds of the investment forward for dollars in the interbank market or going short in that currency in the futures market.

Cross hedge. The hedging of a cash market risk in one commodity or financial instrument by initiating a position in a futures contract for a different but related commodity or instrument. A cross hedge is based on the premise that although the two commodities or instruments are not the same, their prices generally move together.

Current yield. The return on an asset calculated by dividing the annual coupon payments by the current price of the asset. Accrued interest is typically omitted in the calculation.

Daily settlement. The process in a futures market in which the daily price changes are paid by the parties incurring losses to the parties making profits.

Day trading. The intraday trading in securities in which positions are typically closed out by the end of the trading session.

Deferred contracts. Futures contracts that call for delivery in the most distant months, as distinguished from nearby months.

Delivery. The tender and receipt of an actual financial instrument or cash in settlement of a futures contract, or the transfer of ownership or control of the underlying commodity or financial instrument under terms established by the exchange. The possibility that delivery can occur causes cash and futures prices to converge. As the time for delivery approaches, the prices in both markets are about the same.

Delivery factor. See Conversion factor.

Delivery month. A calendar month during which delivery against a futures contract can be made.

Delta. The ratio of the change in an option's price for a given change in the underlying asset or futures price.

Delta/gamma-neutral. A hedge position constructed using a combination of options, futures, and/or the underlying security that has both a net delta and a net gamma of zero for the combined position.

Delta-neutral. A hedge position constructed using a combination of options, futures, and/or the underlying security that has a net delta of zero for the combined position.

Delta/gamma/vega-neutral. A hedge position constructed using a combination of options, futures, and/or the underlying security that has a net delta, gamma, and vega each equal to zero for the combined position.

Dividend yield. The ratio of the dividend to the stock price.

Duration. A measure of the size and timing of a bond's cash flows. It also reflects the weighted average maturity of the bond and indicates the sensitivity of the bond's price to a change in its yield to maturity.

Dynamic hedge. An investment strategy, often associated with portfolio insurance, in which an asset is hedged by selling futures in such a manner that the position is adjusted frequently and simulates a protective put. Other option positions can also be created using dynamic hedging.

Dynamic option replication. The replication of the payoff of an option created by shifting funds appropriately between a risky asset and cash as the risky asset's price changes.

Early exercise. The exercise of an American option before its expiration date.

Effective annual rate. The rate of return of an investment as if compounding occurred annually. The calculation of this rate allows comparison of investments with different compounding frequencies.

Eurodollar. A dollar deposited in a European bank or a European branch of an American bank.

European option. An option that can be exercised only when it expires.

Exercise. To invoke the right granted under the terms of the listed options contact to purchase or sell the underlying security. The holder is the one who can choose to exercise. Call holders exercise to buy the underlying security, while put holders exercise to sell the underlying security.

Exercise price. The price at which an option permits its owner to buy or sell the underlying security, futures, or currency.

Expiration date. The date after which an option or futures contract is no longer effective.

Fair value. Normally, a term used to describe the worth of an option or futures contract as determined by a mathematical model or arbitrage relationship.

Fence. See Collar.

Foreign exchange rate. The rate at which a given amount of one currency converts to another currency.

Forward contract. A transaction in which two parties agree to the purchase or the sale of a commodity at some future time under such conditions as the two agree upon. Those who use forward contracts often expect to make or take physical delivery of the merchandise or financial instrument. Each contract is tailored specifically to the needs of buyer and seller. Trading is generally done by phone in a decentralized marketplace. In contrast to futures contracts, the terms of forward contracts are not standardized; a forward contract is not transferable and usually can be canceled only with the other party's consent, which often must be obtained for consideration and under penalty; forward contracts are not traded in federally designated contract markets.

Forward foreign exchange rate. The rate associated with the purchase or sale of a currency for a specific deferred delivery date; e.g., the amount of dollars necessary to be paid for delivery of Swiss francs in six months.

Forward interest rate. The rate agreed upon in a forward contract for a loan or implied by the relationship between short-term and long-term interest rates.

Futures commission merchant. A firm in the business of executing futures transactions for the public.

Futures contract. An agreement between a buyer and a seller to purchase an asset or currency at a later date at a fixed price. The contract trades on a futures exchange and is subject to a daily settlement procedure.

Futures market. A market in which contracts for the future delivery of commodities or financial instruments are traded. Can refer to a specific exchange or the market in general.

Futures option. An option on a futures contract.

Gamma. The ratio of the change in the option's delta for a given change in the underlying asset or futures price.

Hedge. A transaction in which an investor seeks to protect a current position or anticipated position in the spot market by using an opposite position in options or futures.

Hedge ratio. The ratio of options or futures to a spot position (or vice versa) that achieves an objective such as minimizing or eliminating risk.

Historical volatility. The standard deviation of return on a security, futures, or currency obtained by estimating it from historical data over a recent time period.

Horizontal spread. See Calendar spread.

Implied repo rate. The cost of financing a cash-and-carry transaction that is implied by the relationship between the spot and futures price.

Implied volatility. The standard deviation of return on the underlying security obtained when the market price of an option equals the price given by a particular option-pricing model.

Initial margin. The amount each participant in the futures market must deposit to his margin account at the time a buy or sell order is placed.

Interest rate parity. The relationship between the spot and forward foreign exchange rates and the interest rates in the two relevant countries.

In the money. A call (put) option in which the price of the asset, future, or foreign exchange rate exceeds (is less than) the exercise price.

Intrinsic value. For a call (put) option, the greater of zero or the difference between the security (exercise) price and the exercise (security) price.

Inventory hedge. A long inventory hedge is initiated by buying futures contracts to protect against a rise in the price of an asset currently held in a short position. A short inventory hedge is initiated by selling futures contracts to protect against a fall in the price of an asset currently held in a long position.

Kappa. See Vega.

Last trading day. The final day under exchange rules when trading may occur in a given contract month. Contracts outstanding at the end of the last trading day must be settled by delivery of the underlying commodity or securities or by agreement for cash settlement.

Leverage. The ability to control a large dollar amount of a commodity or cash instrument with a comparatively small amount of capital (margin). In the futures market, the margin is merely a good faith performance bond; in the cash market, the margin is an actual down payment on equity.

LIBOR. The London Interbank Offered Rate. Usually, European banks offer a "scale" of different rates for Eurodollar deposits, which differ for various maturities. As with the prime rate in the United States, the LIBOR may vary from institution to institution.

Limit move. An occurrence in which the futures price hits the upper or lower daily price limit.

Long. As a noun, the term refers to a trader who has purchased an option or futures contract or the cash commodity or financial instrument (depending upon the market under discussion) and has not yet offset that position. As a verb, the term means the action of a trader taking a position in which he has bought options or futures contracts (or a cash commodity) without taking the offsetting action. For example, if a trader has no position and he buys five futures contracts, he is long. If, however, his previous position was one of having sold five contracts to offset that position, his second action would not be referred to as going long because his position when the second action is concluded will be zero.

Maintenance margin. A sum, usually smaller than—but a proportion of—the original margin, that must be maintained on deposit while a position is outstanding. When the equity in an account drops below the maintenance level, the broker issues a margin call requesting that enough money be added to the equity balance to bring it up to the initial margin level.

Margin. An amount of money deposited by both buyers and sellers of futures contracts to ensure performance of the terms of the contract (the delivery or taking of delivery of the commodity or the cancellation in the position by a subsequent offsetting trade). Margin in commodities is not a payment of equity or down payment on the commodity itself but rather is a performance bond or security deposit or "good faith" deposit (also referred to as an initial or original margin).

Mark to market. See Daily settlement.

Maturity. The time in the future when financial contracts fall due or expire.

Maximum price fluctuation (limit move). The maximum amount futures contract prices can move up or down during a specific trading session; e.g., U.S. Treasury bonds may be allowed by the exchange to rise or fall 64/32nds of a point above or below the previous trading day's settlement price.

Mean—variance comparison. A comparison of risk and return for an asset using the mean return and variance (or standard deviation) of return.

Minimum price fluctuation. Also referred to as a point or "tick," the minimum price fluctuation is the smallest allowable increment of price movement in a given contract.

Minimum-variance hedge ratio. The ratio of futures contracts for a given spot position that minimizes the variance of the profit from the hedge.

Modified duration. A duration measure scaled by dividing the original duration by 1 plus the interest rate for the period of compounding.

Money-market rate. The interest rate paid on money market instruments such as certificates of deposit (CDs). The rate is a simple interest rate usually based on a 360-day year for the term of the deposit.

Money spread. An option transaction that involves a long position in one option and a short position in an otherwise identical option with a different exercise price. Also referred to as a vertical spread.

Naked position. An outright long or short position in the cash or futures market that is not hedged, spread, or part of an arbitrage.

National Futures Association. An organization of firms engaged in the futures business that serves as the industry's self-regulatory body.

Nearby contract. The futures contract month trading for the most immediate delivery as distinguished from distant or deferred months.

Negative carry. The net cost incurred when the cost of financing (usually at the repo rate) is greater than the yield on the asset being carried.

Net cost of carry, or net carry. The net cost of financing, which is equal to the cost of financing (usually at the repo rate) minus the yield on the asset being carried.

Offsetting order. A futures or option transaction that is the exact opposite of a previously established long or short position.

Open contracts or positions. Contracts that have been initiated but that have not yet been liquidated or offset by subsequent sale or purchase or by going through the delivery process.

Open interest. The number of futures or options contracts that have been established and not yet offset or exercised.

Open outcry. The auction system used in the trading pits on the floor of the futures exchange. All bids and offers are made openly and loudly by public, competitive outcry and hand signals in such manner as to be available to all members in the trading pit at the same time.

Opening transaction. A trade that adds to the net position of an investor. An opening buy adds more long securities to the account. An opening sell adds more short securities.

Option. A contract to buy or sell an asset, currency, or a futures contract for a fixed price at a specific time.

Option Clearing Corporation. The issuer of all listed option contracts trading on national option exchanges.

Option replication. Techniques used to replicate the payoff of an option. These techniques might involve dynamic hedging or option replication, synthetic option creation, or using a basket of short-term options, futures, and a riskless asset to give a payoff pattern over time similar to a specific option.

Option sensitivity measures. The change in option price or characteristics attributable to changes in the price of the underlying security, interest rates, volatility, and time to expiration. See Delta, Gamma, Rho, Vega, and Theta.

Out of the money. A call (put) option in which the price of the asset, currency, or futures contract is less (greater) than the exercise price.

Overvalued. A condition in which a security, option, or future is priced at more than its fair value.

Payoff. The amount of money received from a transaction at the end of the holding period.

Payoff profile. A graph of an option strategy payoff plotted with respect to the ending security price.

Payout protection. The downward adjustment of the exercise price of an option following a cash distribution from a security (e.g., ex-dividend price decline on stocks)

Pit. A location on the floor of a futures exchange designated for trading a specific contract or commodity.

Portfolio insurance. An investment strategy using combinations of securities, options, or futures that is designed to provide a minimum or floor value of the portfolio at a future date. Equivalent to the payoff of a protective put on the portfolio.

Position limit. The maximum number of contracts that can be held as specified in federal regulations.

Position trading. An approach to trading in which a trader either buys or sells contracts and holds them for an extended period of time, as distinguished from the day trader, who normally initiates and offsets his position within a single trading session.

Positive carry. The net gain earned over time when the cost of financing (usually at the repo rate) is less than the yield on the asset being financed.

Protective put. An investment strategy involving the use of a long position in a put and an asset to provide a minimum selling price for the asset.

Pure discount bond. A bond, such as a Treasury bill, that pays no coupon but sells at a discount from par value.

Put/call/futures parity. The relationship among

the prices of puts, calls, and futures on a security, commodity, or currency.

Put option. An option granting the holder the right to sell the underlying security or currency at a certain price for a specified period of time.

Put/call parity. The relationship between the prices of puts, calls, and the underlying security, commodity, or currency.

Ratio spread. An option strategy in which the ratio of long to short positions is different from 1.

Repo. See Repurchase agreement.

Repurchase agreement. A securities transaction in which an investor sells a security and promises to repurchase it in a specified number of days at a higher price reflecting the prevailing interest rate.

Rho. The ratio of the change in an option price to a change in interest rates.

Riskless asset. An asset with a nominal return that is known with certainty. The return on a short-term Treasury bill is often used as a proxy.

Risk premium. The additional return a risk-averse investor expects for assuming risk. It is often measured as the difference in return over a riskless asset like a Treasury bill.

Rolling. An action in which the investor closes current options or futures currently in the position and opens other options or futures with different strike prices or maturities on the same underlying security.

Securities and Exchange Commission. The federal agency responsible for regulating the securities and options markets.

Settlement price. The price established by a clearinghouse at the close of the trading session as the official price to be used in determining net gains or losses, margin requirements, and the next day's price limits. The term "settlement price" is also often used as an approximate equivalent to the term "closing price."

Sharpe ratio. The ratio of an investment's risk premium to its volatility.

Short. As a noun, the term means a trader who has sold options or futures contracts or the cash commodity (depending upon the market under discussion) and has not yet offset that position. As a verb, the term means the action of a trader taking a position in which he has sold options or

futures contracts or made a forward contract for sale of the cash commodity or instrument.

Short straddle. An option transaction that involves a short position in a put and a call with the same exercise price and expiration.

Simple interest rate. The interest rate used to calculate the interest payment for a specific period of time prorated for the portion of a year the maturity represents.

Spot. The characteristic of being available for immediate (or nearly immediate) delivery. An outgrowth of the phrase "on the spot," it usually refers to a cash market price for stocks or physical commodities available for immediate delivery. Spot is also sometimes used in reference to the futures contract of the current month, in which case trading is still "futures" trading but delivery is possible at any time.

Spot price. The price of an asset on the spot market.

Spread. An option or futures transaction consisting of a long position in one contract and a short position in another, similar contract.

Stack hedge. A hedge constructed by using nearby contracts with the intent to roll them over to deferred contracts when the hedge must be extended in time.

Standard deviation. A measure of the dispersion of a random variable around its mean. It is equal to the square root of the variance.

Stochastic dominance. A mathematical technique used to compare the possible returns from two risky investments. If the probability distribution of asset F dominates that of asset G, an investor would prefer asset F over G.

Stock index. An average of stock prices designed to measure the performance of the stock market as a whole.

Stock index futures. A futures contract on any underlying stock index.

Straddle. An option transaction that involves a long position in a put and a call with the same exercise price and expiration.

Strangle. An option transaction that involves a long position in a call and in a put with the same expiration and for which the strike price of the call exceeds that of the put.

Strike price. See Exercise price.

Strip hedge. A hedge constructed by using contracts of varied maturities in contrast to using all nearby contracts.

Synthetic call. A combination of a long put and a long asset, future, or currency that replicates the behavior of a call. It may sometimes include a short position in risk-free bonds.

Synthetic cash. A combination of a long asset, a short call, and a long put that replicates the return on a riskless asset.

Synthetic futures. A combination of a long call and a short put that replicates the behavior of a long futures contract. It may sometimes include a long position in risk-free bonds.

Synthetic put. A combination of a long call and a short asset, currency, or future that replicates the behavior of a put. It may sometimes include a long position in risk-free bonds.

Term structure of interest rates. The relationship between interest rates and maturities of zero-coupon bonds.

Theta. The negative of the ratio of the change of an option price to a change in expiration date.

Time value. The difference between an option's price and its intrinsic value.

Time value decay. The erosion of an option's time value as expiration approaches.

Treasury bill. Short-term, pure-discount bonds issued by the U.S. government with original maturities of 91, 182, and 365 days.

Treasury bond. A coupon-bearing bond issued by the U.S. government with an original maturity of at least 10 years.

Treasury note. A coupon-bearing bond issued by the U.S. government with an original maturity of 1 to 10 years.

Treynor ratio. The ratio of an investment's risk premium to its beta.

Unbiased. The characteristic of a forecast in which the prediction equals the actual outcome on average over a large number of predictions.

Undervalued. A condition in which a security, option, or futures is priced at less than its fair value.

Underlying security. The security that an investor has the right to buy or sell via the terms of the listed option or futures contract.

Value matrix. A matrix of values to show the payoff of an option strategy above and below the relevant exercise prices of the options used.

Variance. A measure of the dispersion of a random variable around its mean, equal to the square of the standard deviation.

Variation margin. Money added to or subtracted from a futures account that reflects profits or losses accruing from the daily settlement.

Variation margin call. A demand for money issued by a brokerage house to its customer to bring the equity in an account back up to the margin level.

Vega. The ratio of a change in an option price to a change in the volatility of the underlying security. Sometimes referred to as kappa.

Vertical spread. See Money spread.

Volatility. A measure of the amount by which an underlying security is expected to fluctuate in a given period of time. It is generally measured by the annual standard deviation of the daily percentage price changes in the security.

Write. To sell an option. The investor who sells is called a writer.

Yield curve. A chart in which yield to maturity is plotted on the vertical axis and the term to maturity of debt instruments of similar creditworthiness (usually governments) is plotted on the horizontal axis. Similar to a term structure curve.

Yield to maturity. The internal rate of return earned by a debt instrument held to maturity. Capital gains or losses are considered as well as coupon payments. Semiannual compounding is typically assumed.

Zero-coupon bond. See Pure discount bond.